The vision of the Soma Family of Churches is to see gospel saturation, so that every man, woman, and child has a daily encounter with Jesus in word and deed.

We believe the best way to pursue this vision is to establish a family of churches around the world, whose primary life happens in missional community and who are committed to making disciples who make disciples to the glory of God.

WILL YOU PURSUE THIS VISION WITH US?

soⓂⓐSENDING

MAKING DISCIPLES
THROUGH PLANTING CHURCHES TOGETHER
ACROSS NORTH AMERICA & BEYOND

IMMERSION:

> Two school years, practicing Soma life in a Soma Family Church

> Intentional leadership development & personalized coaching

> Hands-on training & assessment in the context of a family of servant missionaries

SUMMITS:

> Seven extended weekends, with a cohort of fellow church planters

> Training & discussion in proven church planting competencies, from some of the best leaders in the U.S.

> Experiential learning, to immediately translate knowledge into practice

APPLICATIONS START EVERY WINTER FOR NEW ROUNDS, WHICH BEGIN EVERY FALL

LEARN MORE & APPLY: SOMASENDING.COM

SENT TOGETHER

How the Gospel Sends Leaders to Start Missional Communities

Brad Watson

— To Bread&Wine's Gospel Community Leaders

TABLE OF CONTENTS

Appendixes

INTRODUCTION

I was riding in the back of an old and noisy Mercedes Benz up and down narrow cobble stone streets in Lisbon, when I realized I was part of a community and it was powerful. Someone was taking an interest in me, there were people who cared for me, there were people who shared life with me, and it made a difference in how I saw Jesus.

One of the leaders in our church was taking me to a bass guitar lesson. He was in his late thirties, a husband, dad, and business owner, yet he was driving me and my kid brother around so we could learn music. He took us into his home with his family and shared more than musical notes with us—he showed me what loving Jesus looked like for a busy business owner and how to use music to worship God. But this was not one-on-one discipleship; this was a community effort. Others in our community would meet up with me to watch movies, others would share requests for healing, and the rest would pray. Financial needs were cared for. Parties were thrown in celebration.

I remember lots of laughter and tears in that community. Above all, I remember Jesus' presence. Being part of that community helped Jesus go from blurry to clear. It wasn't just for me, it was for many. That community of believers called Graça, or "Grace" in English, made Jesus clear to many people. Through that community Jesus made himself known to us and our city. This is the type of community we long for. This is the kind of community our cities need—ones that make the gospel known within and outside of it.

GOOD NEWS IN THE CITY

Our cities are the gathering place of culture, human capital, and change. Suburban flight is a reality as young educated creatives flock to cities for the opportunities and lifestyle it offers. All this

11

comes on the heals of the American church surrendering property and influence in the urban core while finding its place as the religion of the suburbs. Evangelical Christianity doesn't have a literal or cultural place in the city. We gave it up decades ago. Now, we're trying to reengage in a context completely different from the orderly and homogeneous context of the suburbs the church has made its home.

Cities need both worship gatherings and missional communities to intersect the people and needs of the city. This book will focus on the need for missional communities in the city. It is in the context of relationship that the gospel shines brightly, speaks clearly, and welcomes sojourners with questions and doubts.

Oddly, the first step forward isn't toward cutting edge strategies or culturally relevant events. It's pressing into the gospel—the thing of first importance. The gospel is the good news that Jesus has defeated sin, death, and evil through his own death and resurrection and is making all things new, even us. This is good news in the city and for the city.

The city is where death, evil, and destruction is obvious to all. The affects of sin, whether it is acknowledged as sin or not, is exposed in every neighborhood. The city is where the abused gather together. It's where the enslaved, broken, and downtrodden end up. It's where schools fail to keep kids safe. It's where injustice is present on almost every corner. It's where isolation from community, family, and others is rampant. Cities are settling grounds for fugitives and refugees. They gather orphans. They are the last stop for vulnerable women.

The city is also a place for hope. It's where we hope in our humanity, ingenuity, non-profits, and creative solutions. The city is a place of beautiful artwork, music, and cuisine. Cities gather ideas. The city is where humans, created in God's image, thrive in expressing some of God's most beautiful attributes: compassion, mercy, creativity, and justice.

Despite the high volume of humans, each made in God's image, our hopes and solutions always fall short. Despite the population density, one of the biggest needs is loving community. Despite the creative capital, one of the biggest needs is justice and healing. Despite the plethora of opportunities, one of the biggest voids is lasting satisfaction and joy.

The gospel of Jesus is good news in the city. Sin, death, and evil have been defeated by Jesus through the cross and empty tomb. Jesus isn't just defeating. He is recreating, making all things new. This is good news in the cities of unfulfilled promise and expectation of complete restoration. This good news is what every mayoral candidate promises but only Jesus delivers: not only a new city, but a new humanity. The gospel offers redemption, restoration, and renewal.

COMMUNITY AND MISSION IN THE CITY

The gospel saves us from sin and death toward something: unity with God, unity with his people, and the ministry of reconciliation the gospel of Jesus offers. In other words, Jesus calls us to himself, to his community, and sends us on his restorative mission. The gospel is the starting place. The cause for the gathering and scattering of his people on mission.

I've never been around a community that was centered on the gospel that wasn't on mission. A gospel-centered people is a missional people. I've never been around a community that loves one another, that doesn't have Jesus at the middle of everything they do. A gospel-focused people is a missional community. As Jesus transforms us, we are witnesses to it in public, with friends, at work, and in our homes. The gospel makes us, as Paul says, ministers and messengers of reconciliation. God makes his appeal to the world through us! God's mission of reconciliation goes through gospel community—also known as the Church.

If the truth of Christ's life, death, and resurrection isn't woven into the fabric of everything a community does, it has no purpose outside of its own will to make its cities better. Without the gospel at the center, the community has no reason to endure and bare all things together other than its consumeristic pursuit of the ideal community. This is no different in the city.

Our cities need the gospel to be made visible and audible. This is certainly done on Sunday mornings in worship service throughout the city. However, it is just as crucial the gospel become pervasive in the city through God's scattered people. The city needs gospel communities on mission nestled into every crack of the city.

Our cities need communities of people who are learning to follow Jesus together in a way that renews their city, town, village, hamlet, or other space. They don't need fancy community. In fact, missional communities are always a messy collection of everyday citizens who are devoted to Jesus, to one another, to their neighbors, and their city.

This means they invest in each others' lives, calling one another to repent and behold Christ daily. A missional community reorients their activity to center, not on themselves, but on Christ. They struggle forward as in-process-sinners redeemed by the unconditional and infinite grace of God. They share meals, step humbly into the injustice in their city, welcome others into community, and take care of each other.

We see seek to establish thriving communities because we long to see our cities renewed. I pray to see every nook, cranny, and neighborhood filled with life and restoration. Not simply restoration on the outside (with better schools, better housing, better inclusion of all into the thriving culture of a city, and better culture) but restoration on the inside (whole people, present with God, walking with him in every arena of life, sharing in our love for God, loving one another, and loving our city.)

I'm certain that if our cities knew and experienced the power and grace of the gospel everything would change.

FOR THE COMMUNITY WE LONG FOR

This book is for those who find themselves leading communities of all shapes and sizes. It is written to foster your heart for Jesus and the type of community *he* forms and sends. It is written to help you lead people, ever so slightly into all that Jesus has sent us to be *together*. You will find within this book encouragement, clarification, and tools you can immediately implement in your community.

Community leader, you are my hero. You have raised your hand and humbly said: "I want to care for people and play a role in leading them into a relationship with God and others." You probably find yourself leading a group of people with varying interests, passions, idols, beliefs, and problems. You care about each one of them, you are teachable, humble, and have nothing to cling to except the power of the Spirit of God.

This book is written to give you a road map, to be a help to you. My prayer is that, as you read this book, you will consistently put it down and pray. Pray for yourself, pray for your community, and ask and listen to God for direction, peace, and clarity.

WHERE WE'RE HEADED

We will begin with clarifying our motivation for starting and leading missional communities: the gospel. Any other motivation is false and faltering. Any other answer to the question of why—either pragmatics or desire to be different won't last. We begin the book looking at the grand "why" for all of this.

Then we will dive into what exactly a missional community is and what its goals are all about. We will answer the simple question: what does a missional community do? It is one thing to describe an ideal community; it is another thing to describe what that community does.

Then we will shift our attention to the role of a leader in that type of community. What are you signing up for? What is on your plate and what isn't? How do you even know if this is something God has "called" you to do.

Finally, we will dive into the process of starting a missional community. What parts of the process are essential? How do you start well and how do you maintain and grow a community once it is off the ground?

HOW TO USE THIS BOOK

My aim is to teach you how to lead communities in the gospel and on mission. Sprinkled through this book are reflective questions, assignments, and additional resources to further equip you.

- You could use this book as an introduction to the theology, philosophy, and core concepts of a missional community.
- You could use this resources with a small group of leaders preparing to launch missional communities.
- You could also use this book privately as a community group leader who wants to make the shift toward being a missional community.

PART 1:

WHY WE START MISSIONAL COMMUNITIES: GOSPEL MOTIVATION

CHAPTER 1 |

THE GOSPEL SAVES US AND MOTIVATES US

> *"The gospel is not everything that we believe, do, or say. The gospel must primarily be understood as good news, and the news is not as much about what we must do as about what has been done."* — Tim Keller

> *"For by grace you have been saved through faith. And this is not your own doing; it is the gift of God, 9 not a result of works, so that no one may boast. 10 For we are his workmanship, created in Christ Jesus for good works, which God prepared beforehand, that we should walk in them."* — Ephesians 2:8-10

The gospel is the good news that Jesus has defeated sin, death, and evil through his own death and resurrection and is making all things new, even us.

The foundation for community and mission, as well as the actual power for change, is contained in the message of Jesus. The gospel is the motivation for missional community. The gospel is everything God has done for us and our world.

SIN, DEATH, AND EVIL

The gospel is the good news that Jesus defeated sin, death, and evil. Sin is the truth that is so difficult to deny and so easy to prove: all humans fail to be human. In our thoughts, relationships, actions, work, economics, and politics we all fail to live as the image of God—trusting his goodness and obeying his calling. We honor and worship the created things instead of the Creator. We lie, steal, cheat, lust, curse, and make our own way in this world. But Jesus defeated sin.

Death is the epitome fallen life—life as it was *unintended*. This is never more clear than at a funeral. Despite all the nice things we can say about the person we are burying. The sting of death is its total perversion and defeat of life. Death is the culmination and result of sin. But Jesus defeated death.

Jesus has defeated evil. N.T Wright makes this point well in "Evil and the Justice of God"

> *It isn't that the cross has won the victory, so there's nothing more to be done. Rather, the cross has won the victory as a result of which there are now redeemed human beings getting ready to act as God's wise agents, his stewards, constantly worshiping their Creator and constantly, as a result, being equipped to reflect his image into his creation, to bring his wise and healing order to the world, putting the world to rights under his just and gentle rule...*[1]

Evil, according to Augustine, is the absence or lack of good. It is also the culmination of sin and death perpetuated by sin and death. Evil is the darkest of nights and realities that has come into our world. Disease, poverty, abuse, war, violence, the whole lot of it is evil. The world distorted and consumed by evil. Jesus defeated evil.

JESUS' LIFE, DEATH, RESURRECTION

The life of Jesus, as the revelation of God's own character, demonstrates the way things were meant to be and how short humanity falls from that bliss—personally, relationally, psychologically, socially, politically, economically and in every other dimension of life. In Jesus, we see abundant life lived whole and unified with God, animated and sustained by the Holy Spirit. This is the life he came to give through his death and resurrection.

The death of Jesus speaks to how God has personally taken the terrible cost of that failure on himself in the person of

---

1 N. T. Wright. Evil and the Justice of God. Downers Grove, IL: IVP. 139.

Jesus—the shame, humiliation, agony, alienation and especially the consequences of it, both human and divine. The death our sin is destined us for, Jesus died.

Jesus rose from the dead. Jesus was raised. The glorious resurrection of Jesus inaugurates a new creation which has passed through the horrors of sin and death—a new humanity made of Jesus' disciples living in the power of this new life in which sin and death have been defeated on their behalf. It is the fitful beginning of a coming new world in which the conquered power of sin and death will be finally removed.

ALL THINGS NEW, EVEN US

This good news contains both the power for change and the purpose of life. Its power comes from the dynamic of faith (or trust)—the way in which receiving the free love of God in trusting Jesus simultaneously empties our hands from our own destructive attempts to make ourselves right and fills them with an unassailable identity as God's beloved children. As sons and daughters of God, the gospel makes us family.

The purpose of the gospel comes from the dynamic of hope—the restoration of God's creation from humanity's fall through the promised work of Jesus proclaimed in all of life by the church until creation's final restoration. The Gospel makes us ambassadors. The result of that faith and hope is love—for both God and neighbor.

This is how the gospel is motivation: it is the news that re-shapes everything! The Good News is comprehensive, making all things new—bringing about complete restoration, peace, joy, and justice forever. Life as it was supposed to be is possible only through the gospel. Reconciliation of us to God, to each other, and to our neighbor is done through the gospel and expressed in missional community.

The gospel changes everything personally, globally, and eternally. As the New City Catechism asks and answers well in:

"What else does Christ's death redeem? Christ's death is the beginning of the redemption and renewal of every part of fallen creation." — *Question and Answer 26*

REFLECTION&DISCUSSION

The Bible is the best place to begin to understand the message of the gospel, that's what the Bible is. Read the following passages and write down 2-3 key points that summarize that passage and the gospel. Don't be surprised if the same key points continue to emerge!

John 3:16-17
Romans 3:23
Ephesians 2:8-10
Romans 1:16
Galatians 1:8
1 Peter 1:12

Now in one to three sentences, using your own words, answer the question: What is the gospel?

PREPARATION&PLANNING

How does the Good News motivate you in leadership and community?

What are other motivations are possible have for leading and starting communities on mission? What is good or bad about those? How do they compare to the gospel?

How will you regularly remind yourself of the deep motivation of the gospel?

CHAPTER 2 |

THE GOSPEL CHANGES WHAT WE BELIEVE

"If the gospel isn't about transformation, it isn't the gospel of the Bible" — Scott McKnight

Jesus came into Galilee, proclaiming the gospel of God, saying: "The time is fulfilled, and the kingdom of God is at hand; repent and believe in the gospel." — Mark 1:14-15

The reality is, most of us are functional atheists: no one is out there caring for us, no one is coming to our rescue, and this is all there is. Some of us might be functional agnostics: There is a God, I just don't know what he is doing in this messed up world. Still, others are functional deists: God exists but we're on our own to fix ourselves and our world.

All of these beliefs send us into the world to secure our own comfort, acceptance, significance, and satisfaction through our own means or by using other people. Though we might shout, scream, and hope for someone to make us whole, shape our lives, and make us what we long to be, we don't believe anyone can or will. Therefore, we settle for a lesser ambition. Instead of hoping for full restoration and a vibrant life, we hope for a distracted life. We hope for pain relief, instead of healing. We don't believe anyone is coming to our rescue. Even if someone claims to be a savior, we doubt they could change us.

Whether you have thrown yourself into religious activity or rejected religion as a fraud to flee, outside of the gospel, you believe this is all there is and it's up to you, others, or things to make some sort of life for yourself to fight the battles of this world on your own. At the very least, you can somehow work to hold off its evil and win small battles.

Dave Eggers' *What is the What*, a biography of the lost boys of Sudan, provides an extraordinary picture of this. This gripping biography, written like a novel, leaps back and forth from the young man's life as a refugee in America and his story of becoming an orphan in the conflict of southern Sudan. One of the most heart-griping scenes takes place in his Atlanta apartment after someone has knocked him out, tied him to a chair, and stolen all his worthwhile possessions. Achek finds himself alone in a foreign country, beaten, bleeding, and desperate for help. He bangs his feet and head on the floor. After hours of banging, he begins to repeat this phrase to himself: "no one is coming."

This is how we live, feel, and groan for something. How can they not hear? When are they coming? No one is coming . . . despite my efforts, pain, purchasing of things, efforts in my career, controlling of my children, love for my spouse, this world will consume me. I'm alone, rejected, and destined for heart ache.

THE GOSPEL IS DOCTRINAL

This is the first major change the gospel brings. The gospel changes what we believe about life, pain, death, and rescue. The gospel is the good news that Jesus has defeated sin, death, and evil through his death and resurrection and is making all things new, even us. This news demands a change of belief. This is earth shattering and reshaping news:

- God came to rescue
- God defeated sin, evil, and death for us
- God took on pain, suffering, and death
- God is victorious in life
- God loves us and comes to us.

This means we no longer struggle to make ourselves right and justify our actions before ourselves, others, or God. Instead we find our justification in him. Instead of trying to find something worthy of our worship in this world, we worship the

God who saves and brings life out of death. Instead of fearing death, we behold life. Instead of securing comfort, we run to our comforter. Instead of striving, we find rest in God. The gospel changes everything we believe and therefore how we live.

THE GOSPEL IS HISTORY MAKING NEWS

Instead of thinking we are alone to justify ourselves, the gospel is something that happened and evidences God's grace, mercy, and power to defeat death and bring life.

Throughout history there were other gospel proclamations. The word gospel simply means important, heralded news. Perhaps most commonly used as the message shared by those coming from the battle field to update the villages and towns: "The king has won and defeated the enemy! All is well and the war is over and we can enter peace." The gospel is a news worthy event that must be and is shared. There are other proclamations of great victories. However, Jesus' is the ultimate.

> *"Now I would remind you, brothers, of the gospel I preached to you, which you received, in which you stand, and by which you are being saved, if you hold fast to the word I preached to you—unless you believed in vain. For I delivered to you as of first importance what I also received: that Christ died for our sins in accordance with the Scriptures, that he was buried, that he was raised on the third day in accordance with the Scriptures, and that he appeared to Cephas, then to the twelve." — 1 Corinthians 15:1-5*

The gospel of "first importance" is the historic claim that Jesus Christ lived, died, was buried, and rose from the dead for our sins in the first century A.D. Notice, this *happened*. These events were anticipated in the Old Testament, witnessed in the first century, recorded in the New Testament, and attested by contemporary historians. In short, this history-making news demands a shift of belief and is only truly understood when it is held as primary.

THE GOSPEL IS CHRIST CENTERED NEWS

Instead of life being centered on us, our needs, and our attempts to make life manageable, the gospel is centered on Jesus.

> *Jesus says, "I am the resurrection and the life. Whoever believes in me, though he die, yet shall he live, and everyone who lives and believes in me shall never die." — John 11:25-26*

The gospel asks us to believe that Jesus died our deserved death (for our sins) and that he rose from the dead to give us his undeserved life (for our salvation). Notice that the "belief" required is not in an idea but in a person: "whoever believes in me." Jesus isn't asking us to merely agree with a doctrine, but to trust him for undeserved forgiveness and life. The gospel is Christ-centered.

The gospel is history-making, Christ-centered news that is so significant it bears believing and announcing. The doctrinal aspect of the gospel makes specific claims, grounded in historical events, which must be believed to know Christ and receive his saving forgiveness. The gospel is not one spiritual idea among many. It is exclusive and unique in its claims because Jesus has uniquely done what no one else can do (Acts 4:12; 1 Tim. 2:5-9)!

The doctrinal gospel changes what we believe. This is why we start and live in missional communities. We do so to spur each other on. We are motivated by Christ's sufficient work!

Many times, leaders forget this. We operate in the mode that we are all alone trying to making people's lives better. We are tying to make those we lead. We are in charge. In reality, the "news" we are sharing is "leader-centered". The underlying belief or message is: everyone who needs help, come to me (the leader), and I will fix you. We operate in a way, too, where God is absent, distant, or non-existent. Leaders must regularly remind themselves and return to belief in the gospel's power to save and make all things news.

REFLECTION&DISCUSSION

How does your life reflect what you believe? What, looking at your life, priorities, values, and spending, do you believe?

What elements of the gospel are hard to believe for you? Which elements are easier?

How does the gospel's historical and Christ-centered message motivate you to lead a missional community?

PREPARATION&PLANNING

When things get difficult how will the gospel motivate you to persevere?

How will you be reminded or remind yourself of the gospel?

What are some regular practices, you as a leader can do to check your heart and beliefs and pursue a renewal of your mind in the gospel?

CHAPTER 3 |

THE GOSPEL CHANGES WHO WE ARE

Many of us find meaning in who we are, where we come from, what we do for a living, or where we live. The list is long and we try to squeeze that significance, or the best of us, into our 140-character bio. We label ourselves, we are labelled by others, and our cultures tells us to find and express ourselves. It's all quite confusing, disorienting, and we are left clinging to mishmash of views or stories about ourselves. This mosaic forms our identity.

My family moved to Lisbon, Portugal a two weeks after I turned eleven. Upon arrival we had to go through a long processes of becoming legal residents. We had just landed in a beautiful country we knew hardly anything about. They spoke a language we didn't know and everything operated in a rhythm of life with deep currents we weren't privy to. All this was an exciting adventure for an eleven year old until it came time to stand in line at the immigration office.

The line grew from the office down stairs and around the block. We were standing there with Eastern Europeans, Africans, and South Americans. I had spent my entire life feeling at home. This was the first time I didn't. Etched into my identity from that moment on was the label "Estrangeiro" — stranger, foreigner. It became an identity I that shaped many of my actions and thoughts as something I was ashamed of and wanted to compensate for and as something I was proud of and committed to. The event of moving to Portugal changed me.

THE GOSPEL IS PERSONAL

The gospel doesn't simply transform our minds and hearts in our belief, the gospel changes who we are. The gospel is personal. The historically rooted, world changing news of Jesus makes you new. The gospel changes your identity *and* your character.

THE GOSPEL CHANGES YOUR IDENTITY
We are Now Sons and Daughters of God

The Scriptures describe a transformation from Orphan to Son or Daughter of God. We are adopted into the family of God by God's grace. Though we were once alone and estranged from our father in heaven, God relentless sought to bring you back into the family. The New Testament calls believers in Jesus heirs—sons and daughters of God, brothers and sisters in Christ. No longer do we live as orphans in this world left to control, manipulated, and grasp for security admits chaos. We now receive the blessing and position of being God's beloved.

We are Now Free Friends of God

The New Testament is also straight forward in the transformation from slave of sin to liberated friend of God. The gospel is the message that we have now been purchased, ransomed, and liberated from the power of sin by Christ's death and resurrection. The gospel liberates us from the identity of slave in this world to free-man. Sitting around the table with his disciples as he prepared for his death, he speaks eloquently to those who have followed his ministry most closely: "I no longer call your servants, I know call you friends." Jesus came to establish friendship between us and God. His death is the way for us to be reconciled and freed in to be in union with Christ.

We are Now Citizens of the Kingdom of God

From Refugee to Citizen of the Kingdom of God. We were once of the kingdom of darkness, aliened and estranged from God. Now have been transferred into the kingdom of glorious light. No longer do we scavenge for a place in this world. No longer are we resigned to being our own king. Instead, we have found our home in Jesus our king and our lives are shaped by life in his kingdom of compassion, grace, forgiveness, love, and hope.

When our motivation for leading communities comes from a desire to see people remember who God redeemed them to be, we don't control them. When our desires are rooted, as Paul describes, "being complete *in* Christ," we are able to pursue Christ in leading.

Becoming Like Jesus

Outside of the gospel reality we are destined to self-help and improvement projects. It's hard and exhausting work. Sometimes we see results, but rarely does it transform even part us. The gospel promises to change you entirely.

> *"Therefore, if anyone is in Christ, he is a new creation. The old has passed away; behold, the new has come. All this is from God, who through Christ reconciled us to himself and gave us the ministry of reconciliation; that is, in Christ God was reconciling the world to himself, not counting their trespasses against them, and entrusting to us the message of reconciliation." — 2 Corinthians 5:17-19*

The gospel changes us into the image and likeness of Jesus. Paul tells us that this gospel change happens by keeping our eyes on Jesus. It does not happen by keeping our eyes on our failure. The gospel frees us to admit our failures, because our worth doesn't hang on our success. Rather, our worth hangs on Jesus' success, his life over death. We can confess our sins without fear of judgment because Jesus has borne our judgment for us. As a result, for every look at sin we should look ten times at Christ—where we are reminded that Jesus is our forgiveness and acceptance before the Father. This kind of Jesus is worth beholding

The gospel offers hope because it gives us the eyes to behold Jesus as well as the power to become like him. The power for gospel change is the person of the Holy Spirit. The Spirit turns our eyes away from sin and toward our Savior. Because of the Spirit, we are transformed into the image of Jesus' glory:

> *"Beholding the glory of the Lord, are being transformed into the same image from one degree of glory to another. For this comes from the Lord who is the Spirit" — 2 Corinthians 3:17-18*

To be sure, becoming like Jesus is a life-long endeavor. This is why Paul mentions that we are changed "from one degree of glory to another." Our change is incremental and progressive. If we continue to look to Jesus, we will inevitably become like him.

The gospel changes who we are by changing what we look at. We become like Jesus because we behold Jesus. In summary, imperfect disciples cling to a perfect Christ while being perfected by the Spirit. Gospel change isn't perfection overnight but perseverance over a lifetime.

TRANSFORMATION TOGETHER

God uses purposeful community to transform our hearts. The gospel, in the context of a community trying to do something, challenges our hearts and lives. This happens because we are placed in a situation where we are called to repentance, faith, and obedience. This is the process many of us disregard when we isolate and live for ourselves.

You are not saved by the power of the gospel into isolation, but into a people—a community. I will discuss community in depth in chapter six.

DISCUSSION&REFLECTION

Read 1 Peter 2:9-17

- What happens to those who believe in these passages?
- Of the identity statements (for example: "royal priesthood" or "holy nation") which are appealing and difficult for you? Why?
- How does our behavior connect to what God has done?
- How do we become holy? How do we live the kind of life described in verses 13-17?
- How would you put the personal gospel in your own words? How does the gospel change who you are?
- How does this aspect of the gospel motivate you to lead?
- What is the difference between telling people who they are (identity) and telling people how they are supposed to live (duty)? What is your tendency as a leader?

PREPARATION&PLANNING

Spend some time thinking of ways you can teach this aspect of the gospel to your community. Also, think of ways your community could 'practice' or live out your identity.

CHAPTER 4 |

THE GOSPEL CHANGES WHERE WE LIVE

"I am convinced that belief in the gospel leads us to care for the poor and participate actively in our culture, as surely as Luther said true faith leads to good works." — *Timothy Keller*

"Missionary activity is nothing else and nothing less than an epiphany, or a manifesting of God's decree, and its fulfillment in the world and in world history, in the course of which God, by means of mission, manifestly works out the history of salvation." — *Vatican II, Ad Gentes*

Six years ago my wife and I, and several close friends sat in the living room of our first tiny two bedroom duplex on one of Portland's historically artistic streets. We had moved at great cost to the city and were hopeful of how God would use us. We were just beginning to draw out and pray what God was leading us to do. We wanted to see the miraculous: a city transformed by the gospel.

As a group, we talked about how that might happen and what God was asking us to do. We realized our strategy would encompass our entire life, work, recreation, rest, shopping, eating, and service. Then, as we pursued a changed city, we realized the only lasting motivation was rooted in our faith that Jesus was making all things new, even Portland. We found that the gospel was not only sufficient motivation for mission but the means of mission: God is making all things new, even Portland.

The gospel changed how we looked at our city. The gospel changed how we participated in it. We've seen communities birthed in Portland doing things like this: fostering and adopting children, caring for refugees, creating community in apartments, building bridges of reconciliation on streets, hosting parties for others, sharing the gospel with co-workers, starting businesses that change energy uses, and planting therapy gardens for middle schoolers. This is only the tip of the spear.

THE GOSPEL IS MISSIONAL

When the gospel changes what we believe and who we are, it also changes where we live. The gospel goes to us and through us to transform the world around us. We should make great culture, redeem social ill, and share a whole gospel. Christians should be among the most creative, neighborly, and compassionate people in the city. If the gospel truly affects everything, then it should affect everything in our lives including where we live.

If we just focus on the doctrinal and personal aspect of the gospel, we will neglect its missional aspect. If the doctrinal gospel changes what we believe, and the personal gospel changes who we are, then the missional gospel changes where we live and what we say. It is the hopeful announcement that God is making all things new in Christ Jesus! The gospel ushers us into a new kingdom and new world. We no longer live in a world dominated by death and deconstruction but in a world of resurrection and recreation!

> *"The Spirit of the Lord is upon me, because he has anointed me to proclaim good news to the poor. He has sent me to proclaim liberty to the captives and recovering of sight to the blind, to set at liberty those who are oppressed, to proclaim the year of the Lord's favor." — Luke 4:18-19, Isaiah 61*

Not only is this good news for us, but also for our neighbors, the poor, our city, and the world. It affects the social, cultural, and physical fabric of the universe. In Luke 4, Jesus preached the gospel to the poor, marginalized, and oppressed. It is good news for them because through his death and resurrection he has defeated sin, death, and evil (1 John 2:13; 3:8). The gospel announces the in-breaking reign of Jesus, which is in the process of reversing the order of things. The poor become rich, the captives are freed, and the old become new.

THE GOSPEL SENDS US ON MISSION

Those who follow Jesus join his mission by making disciples of all ethnic groups and going, teaching, and baptizing (Matt. 28:18-20). We are sent to teach, speak, counsel, discuss, and proclaim the gospel to others so that they might be baptized into God's new creation and join his mission of making all things new. We are called "ambassadors of reconciliation" and given the privilege of sharing in Jesus' ministry of reconciling the world to himself (2 Cor. 5:17-20). Those who have been changed by the gospel share its life-changing power with others.

We should announce *and* embody the good news by caring for the poor and rebuilding cities (Is. 61:4). In fact, the future for the people of God is an entirely new city in a new creation (Rev. 21). The church should be a movie trailer of this grand, coming attraction, when all things will be made new!

The result of the church—you, us—being sent is that we live as a community of disciples—not only devoted to Jesus and to one another—but devoted to our neighbors and our city, too. When we come to Christ, we are all sent on his mission.

Mission is not an option for followers of Jesus, or something reserved for "super-spiritual or radical Christians." Mission is for everybody! The mission of making disciples who make good culture, redeem social ill, and share a whole gospel is the joy and responsibility of every Christian.

We Participate by Making Disciples

In Matthew 28:18-20 we get to overhear Jesus' parting words to his disciples, who were the beginning of the first missional community:

> *"And Jesus came and said to them, 'All authority in heaven and on earth has been given to me. Go therefore and make disciples of all nations, baptizing them in the name of the*

Father and of the Son and of the Holy Spirit, teaching them to observe all that I have commanded you. And behold, I am with you always, to the end of the age.'" —Matthew 28:18-20

Jesus gives his disciples the life-long purpose of making disciples of Jesus. It isn't a side job or a hobby, but an all encompassing orientation for life. As a disciple, you are called to make disciples of Jesus. Meaning, as you learn to follow Jesus, you invite others to join you by making the gospel clear and tangible. As the God transforms you in and through the power of the Spirit, you humbly challenge others to believe and engage this process. You are, as Eugene Peterson writes, "God's billboard."

We Participate by Loving the Poor

God's mission is also to the oppressed, captive, orphan, and neglected. From the onset of God's mission through his people beginning with Abraham and moving through Moses, David, and the prophets of the Old Testament, God called them to care for those tossed aside. They were to care for the orphan and the oppressed, the sojourner or alien traveling through their lands. It was not simply traditional middle eastern hospitality; it was a command of God, as God's people, to care for those in need, to usher into our broken earth, the grace and love that inhabits heaven.

This clearly, doesn't stop with Jesus. Jesus forgave sins *and* healed sickness. He welcomed those sent to the margins of society to eat with him. He cared for those burdened, ignored, and abused. Jesus proclaimed the gospel and the kingdom of God coming to us. Jesus came for the poor and powerless—the oppressed.

Therefore, Jesus' church is sent on the mission of declaring the gospel and demonstrating the gospel. In other words, as the church spreads and grows by making disciples, it also cares for the poor. A clear mark of a church as early as Pentecost, has been meeting the needs of the marginalized. From the Old Testament through the early Church, God has sent his people on the mission of doing justice *and* inviting the world to experience the God of grace and mercy.

It is almost silly to separate the mission in two parts. One cannot make disciples without caring for the poor, and one cannot care for the poor without making disciples. These are not two distinct missions of God—but the same mission of restoration and recreation of all things.

The Gospel Sends Community on Mission

The gospel is the good news that Jesus has defeated sin, death, and evil through his own death and resurrection and is making all things new, even us. The gospel changes what we believe (doctrinal), who we are (personal), and where we live (missional). Through this gospel transformation, community is created and sent on mission.

A missional community exists because of the gospel and is a group of people that love to include Jesus in everything they do. It never feels forced, but a meal with friends often drifts towards conversation about the person and life of Jesus. If missional community can be characterized by anything it will be characterized by who Jesus is and what he has done for us. His life, work, and character is woven into the language and practice of every authentic expression of community.

Missional communities in whatever shape, language, context, all exist for this end: to live out our faith in the gospel and the implications of the gospel. This is why we start them, lead them, and dedicate so much energy to supporting their growth. The good news of Jesus is what makes the community, builds it, and motivates it.

REFLECTION&DISCUSSION

Theologian Lesslie Newbigin wrote:

> *"The gospel isn't just the illustration of an idea. It's the story of actions by which the human situation is irreversibly changed."*

This is a powerful quote. How often do we think of the gospel as simply an idea about God and not a reality. What areas of your life is the gospel simply an idea? How does the gospel irreversibly change your life and your human situation?

Daniel Montgomery also contributes to this conversation:

> *"The gospel transfers us from the familiar territory of self-centered living into a glorious wilderness, a beautiful and strange place where we're invited to explore the wonders of who God is and what he's done."*

How does the gospel change where you live?

Where is God inviting you to explore the wonders of who is and what he's done?

What is it like to leave the territory of self-centered living and engage the kingdom of God?

PLANNING&PREPARATION

It is important as a leader to be able to explain to the mission of God. Spend some time thinking and writing out what the mission of God is in your own words.

THE GOSPEL CHANGES US: MATT'S STORY OF MISSIONAL COMMUNITY

I met Matt at a poker game. It was a mishmash of people and he was obviously nervous to be around so many new folks. He was going to law school and was the smartest guy in the room. The next time we hung out he was eating dinner at my house. Our missional community was getting together for a meal and sharing stories of what God had done in our lives. He had just heard the gospel from the guy who hosted the poker game and he was beginning to make sense of the death and resurrection of Jesus.

The next day we shoveled fertilizer together at the elementary school as part of a neighborhood wide clean-up project. He wanted to know how to pray to Jesus. Matt became part of our community and began spending lots of life with us. I got to baptize him about six months later.

As we spent time together and he grew in his understanding of the gospel, he shared that he came to our city as a refugee, not as a student. He was running from home and the destructive life he had there. As he read the parable of the prodigal son, he couldn't help but identify with him. "I messed so much stuff up," he would say. At the age of twelve, he gave his life to drugs. It truly stole his life. No friends, no community, and ultimately his family gave up on him. Yet, at 26, Matt was a new man in Jesus.

Three months later, he took an internship at an Indian reservation in another state seven hours away. He took a stack of books and planned to finish reading the Bible (he read two thirds of it in his first months following Jesus). We prayed for him and talked as often as we could and were planning on having several of the guys in the community take a weekend trip to hang out with him.

At 11:00 pm on the fourth of July, we got a phone call from Matt. He was in trouble and me and another leader of our community left immediately. It was the longest seven-hour drive of our life as we tried to piece together the short and chaotic phone calls we had with Mark in the early hours of the morning. We couldn't figure out if he was in real danger or hallucinating. There was a stretch of four hours when we heard nothing from him. As we pulled into the town we found him surrounded by three police cars in a diner parking lot. He had spent the night outside running from terrifying and accusative hallucinations. He was barefoot and his pajamas were torn to pieces. His hands and feet were scarred and bleeding. But he was alive and recognized us.

The police allowed us to take him into our care. We cleaned him up, packed his bags, cleaned his apartment, and brought him home. The coming days and weeks were hard, but he had a community around him who gave him a place to stay, took him to the hospital, fed him, and spoke the truth of resurrection to him. We paid his debts for him and cared for his heart.

Matt's words when he was baptized were true: "Before Christ I was headed no where, I didn't have any friends and did a bunch of bad stuff I felt shame about. Now I have a new life, a community to love and justice to do." Matt was led to Christ, discipled, and cared for by a large cloud of community, not one person. The gospel changes everything.

PART 2:

WHAT MISSIONAL COMMUNITIES DO: LIVE THE GOSPEL

MISSIONAL COMMUNITY DEFINED

A missional community is a way to organize the church to gather and send groups of people on a common mission. Simply put, missional communities are a group of people who are learning to follow Jesus together in a way that renews their city, town, village, hamlet, or other space.

They aren't fancy. In fact, they can be a pretty messy community of everyday citizens who are devoted to Jesus, to one another, and to their neighbors and city.

They are multi-focused: internally and externally driven. They share burdens with one another *and* spur each other on to love the city. Missional communities are groups of people committed to the process of growing in their love for God, one-another, and neighbor.

A missional community has three equal and codependent pursuits:
1. Grow in Our love for God (Gospel Enjoyment)
2. Grow in our love for one-another (Community)
3. Grow in our love to our neighbors and city (Mission)

It is through these pursuits we begin to live lives that reflect our belief in the gospel. We live the gospel.

CHAPTER 5 |

GOSPEL ENJOYMENT: GROWING IN OUR LOVE FOR CHRIST TOGETHER

"Save us, O Lord our God,
and gather us from among the nations,
that we may give thanks to your holy name
and glory in your praise."
— Psalm 106:47

Missional communities exist to grow in love for God. Missional communities are groups of people that learn to follow Jesus. These communities consist of disciples, meaning people are being renewed by the gospel through abiding in Christ. Missional communities are environments to pursue knowing God and the power of his resurrection with others *and* for others.

"LOVE THE LORD YOUR GOD"

"And one of the scribes came up and heard them disputing with one another, and seeing that he answered them well, asked him, "Which commandment is the most important of all?" Jesus answered, "The most important is, 'Hear, O Israel: The Lord our God, the Lord is one. And you shall love the Lord your God with all your heart and with all your soul and with all your mind and with all your strength.' The second is this: 'You shall love your neighbor as yourself.' There is no other commandment greater than these." — Mark 12:28-31

This is the golden rule or greatest commandment: to love. This is what we were created for and this is the cornerstone of all

Christian and Jewish ethics. As Paul writes, "If I don't have love, I have nothing." (1 Cor. 13:1-3).

Love is the only complete reaction to the gospel and expression of the gospel. It was love that motivated God to save us (Jn. 3:16) and love that motivated God's rich mercy towards us (Eph. 2:4). It is love that we receive in the gospel and it is love that we give because of the gospel. As God pours his love out to his people, the only natural response is holistic love and devotion for him. This is the worship our hearts, minds, souls, and bodies were created to give. God is the one we were meant to direct that love towards.

God demands our affections because he is the only one sufficient to receive them. We are commanded to shift our entire being from love of self to love of God. The gospel requires we relinquish all other idols and masters and give ourselves to Jesus as the one true God.

GROWING IN OUR LOVE THROUGH LISTENING

The beginning of Jesus' answer is not "Love God" but "Hear! The Lord Your God is One." This timeless command starts with a proper orientation of who God is and of *listening* to who he is.

A missional community pursues growth in its love for God first by beholding God with wonder, awe, reverence, and need. A missional community focuses on hearing and remembering who God is. The beginning of loving God is a desperate attempt to wade through doubts to discover God himself.

Reading the Scriptures Together

A community will not grow in love for God if it refuses to open, read, and ingest the Word of God. It cannot be a footnote or a side-bar. A community that has any ambition to be more than a dinner club, must come humbly to the Bible as the necessary source of understanding who God is. We grow in our devotion to God by putting ourselves under what he has already spoken and revealed.

The Scriptures carry divine authority. Unlike anything that can be said or spoken, the Bible carries weight. The Spirit works through Scripture like lightening through steel to electrify our faith. It is fundamental to forging conviction and worship.

Ways to Begin Reading the Bible as a Community

- Read one of the Gospels together, asking questions about what is challenging and appealing about Jesus. Who is he and what is he doing? How are people responding to him? How do we respond to him?
- Read through a letter in the New Testament asking four simple questions: Who is God? What is *he* saying about *himself, his* work, and *his* people? What passage do we need to meditate on, remember, and believe.
- Memorize a Psalm together.
- Have a shared reading plan.
- Get into small groups of two's or three's to do more study and in-depth discussion on the Scriptures.
- Follow the Christian Calendar (Advent, Lent, Easter, Pentecost, etc.) using the themes and Scriptures as a guide.
- Follow a simple curriculum. NT Wright's "For Everyone" series and John Stott's guides are excellent.

Praying Together

Paul Miller writes: "Prayer is a moment of incarnation – God with us." But it doesn't feel that way. Communal prayer is awkward. We don't know what to do, and we don't know what to say. We don't know how honest to be. Furthermore, our prayers are not about God or his presence with us but about us. We typically pray with ourselves and our current felt needs as the focal point. We do this because we are the focal point! To grow in our love for God our prayers must center on God. Our gaze has to move from ourselves to the one who holds all things together. This is the only way to begin a praying life. Then, when we bring our concerns to God, we are able to acknowledge his presence in the details of our lives and his power to love us in them.

Take a quick survey of Paul's prayers and you will find overwhelming evidence that Paul doesn't pray for sick grandparents, stress free trips to the super-market, acceptance into good colleges, or even good jobs. Paul was praying for increased love, greater understanding of God's love for us, power, thanksgiving for belief, changed hearts, power to defeat sin, joy, peace, and prophecy—among other things. Paul was praying in light of the gospel and for the gospel to advance in and through the church. These are inspiring prayers and they are unifying prayers because Paul's gaze was not toward the earth but toward heaven. Paul was praying for heaven to break into our everyday struggles, not for the struggles.

Ways to Begin Praying as a Community
- "Pray the Bible"—Read a passage of scripture together, lead people to pray different phrases in their own words or respond to the passage in prayer.
- Lectio Divina (Divine Reading)—an ancient Benedictine prayer format using the Bible. Calls for the group to reflect and meditate on the passage, respond in prayer, then rest in silence.

Tips for Praying in Community
- Have everyone pray short prayers (the sermon-prayer is no fun).
- Have everyone pray in their own voice (no spiritual whispers, please).
- Allow for silence (It's okay if no one is talking. God is present).
- When people bring up their struggles and concerns about life, regardless of the degree, ask if you can pray for that as a group and do it together. Offer the details of life to God. Pray for God's grace, love, and mercy to be known in the trial.

GROWING IN OUR LOVE FOR GOD THROUGH CONFESSION

Confession is the act of "saying the same thing as God" or naming reality. We grow in our love for God by being honest about who we are and how we live. We lower the facade and tell the truth: "We are not a peaceful community," "I don't like serving the poor," or "I don't believe God is concerned or cares for me."

This is how we bring our true selves before God. In fact, Jesus was not too welcoming to the self-righteous and the hiding. Jesus says that he came for the sick in need of a doctor. The only pre-requisite for joining Jesus' entourage was to be honest with who you were: a human tainted by sin. Jesus ate with sinners. Jesus forgave sinners.

Ironically, Christian communities have become hiding places for sinners to pretend they don't need Christ. But we cannot grow in our love for God (with all our hearts, minds, strength), until we tell the truth about our hearts, minds, and strength. This is the beginning of transformation.

Confession is not just about speaking about how bad we or our circumstances are, but about speaking to God about how good God is in our circumstances. Confession is also about saying the truth about God—who he is and what he has done.

King David was the confession expert. He offered God his true feelings of fear, anger, resentment, disappointment, and doubt to God while simultaneously speaking of God's great works, kindness, and power. Our language of God as a "Rock" and "Refuge" comes directly from David's confessions and songs. God was his Rock because David confessed his life was on shaking soil and in need saving and God was the only one who could save him. God was David's refuge because David confessed he couldn't find rest anywhere else in the world—despite his trying. The Psalms show us how to worship God in "spirit and in truth" (Jn. 4:24).

Ways to Practice Confession as a Missional Community

Read a Psalm of confession together (Psalms 6, 32, 38, 51, 102, and 130) and guide your community through each stanza or verse. For example, in Psalm 6.

- Part 1 (vs. 1-3): What causes restlessness in you? What troubles you?
- Part 2 (vs 4-5): What deliverance/salvation do you need from God?

- Part 3 (vs. 6-7): What grieves you? What makes your soul tired?
- Part 4 (vs.8-10): Repeat these verses out loud. God has heard, God hears. God hears our request. God accepts our prayers; he longs to hear them. How has God conquered the enemy and put them to shame? How has God defeated sin? How have you experienced his steadfast love?

GROWING IN OUR LOVE THROUGH REPENTANCE AND FAITH

When you consider who God is and who you really are, you will be confronted by your sin and God's forgiveness. As you press into his glorious grace and taste his kindness, you will hear the call of Jesus in Mark 1:14-15. When Jesus preached the gospel he demanded a response—repent and believe:

> *"Now after John was arrested, Jesus came into Galilee, proclaiming the gospel of God, and saying, 'The time is fulfilled, and the kingdom of God is at hand; repent and believe in the gospel.'"*

When Jesus said "repent" he was saying to turn away not only from sin, but to turn from the lies that sin deceives us with, and to turn towards something truer and better, to turn to Jesus and his true promises. You cannot separate repentance from faith. To repent is reorient your faith. To have faith in Jesus requires a drastic change of direction.

You trust Jesus' incarnation, his kingdom, and his purposes. As a disciple, you exchange your agenda for his. You let go of your imaginary kingdom for his tangible reign. N.T. Wright describes repentance and belief this way in *The Challenge of Jesus*, "[Jesus] was telling his hearers to give up their agendas and to trust him for his way of being Israel, his way of bringing the kingdom, his kingdom-agenda."

Take the deceptive promise of pride, for example. Pride says: "Find and cherish compliments and then you will be confident." But the gospel says, "Instead of trusting in compliments for confidence, believe that your sufficiency comes from God in Christ." 2 Corinthians 3:4-6:

> *"Such is the confidence that we have through Christ toward God. Not that we are sufficient in ourselves to claim anything as coming from us, but our sufficiency is from God, who has made us competent."*

The gospel says: "Your confidence comes, not from your sufficiency, but from God who has made you sufficient in Jesus." Faith in the person of Jesus, who he is and what he has accomplished for us, is true saving, changing faith.

Ways to Grow in Repentance and Faith Together

- As a community, have regular times to reflect together. Ask: Where have we we, as a group, put our trust in things that are not Jesus? Where are we experiencing God's kindness? Do you think we are drawing nearer to God or running away from God?
- Another way to have this communal discussion is to ask questions along the lines of motive for obedience: Are we doing it as a performance (religion)? Are we doing it to follow the rules or model (legalism)? Are we becoming obedience because we see God' love more clearly (sanctification)?

THE MISSION IS TO BE RECONCILED TO GOD

You might associate missional community with local involvement, justice, and neighborhood evangelism. You're likely attracted to books like this because you want to live out the cause of Christ in a tangible way. However, you *are* God's mission. Christ came to save you, and for you to be reconciled to God. This is the substance of living the gospel.

Many leaders and missional communities forget they are supposed to enjoy God, know his love, and grow in loving him. We forget that we are God's mission *and* on God's mission. You and your community were created to live the gospel in unity with God. To taste the grace of God through repentance and faith. To worship God through confession. To know the depth of God's love by listening to God.

"Mission is an acted out doxology. That is its deepest secret. Its purpose is that God may be glorified." — Lesslie Newbigin

Never forget that one of the primary goals of your missional community is to increasingly grow towards Christ.

REFLECTION&DISCUSSION

Read John 15:1-11. What does it mean to abide in God's love? Who do you abide in?

Using this passage have a time of prayer, confession, repentance, and worship.

PREPARATION&PLANNING

What is missing in your community? How does your group focus on the gospel through reading and prayer?

What regular practices do you think would be important?

What would you like to implement from the beginning?

CHAPTER 6 |

COMMUNITY: GROWING IN OUR LOVE FOR ONE ANOTHER

"A new commandment I give to you, that you love one another: just as I have loved you, you also are to love one another. By this all people will know that you are my disciples, if you have love for one another." — John 13:34-35

"We live together because we are conceived together, in Christ. As a result, every Christian upon conversion is called into God's community. There are no exceptions. No one is left out. Everyone has a place in the people of God." — Jonathan Dodson

In the last chapter, we focused on Jesus' reiteration of an old commandment. This chapter shifts toward a new one. You will not find a more beautiful picture of a "missional community" meal than the one John writes in his Gospel from chapters 13 through 17. Jesus serves and cleans his disciples feet, clarifying they are his friends and not his servants. He prays for his disciples and the impact they will make on the world. The whole occasion is filled with God's love for this random band of brothers and the world they are sent to love.

This is what I wish every missional community meal was like in my home—completely centered on Christ. This is the clearest picture of Christ-centered community in the Bible. They were together because Christ had interrupted their lives. The benchmark for acceptance into this community was allowing Jesus to wash and serve each of them. They were free to ask questions and to err; however, they were graciously turned towards God, his love, and his purpose in this world.

The command Jesus gives in this moment cannot be ignored: love one-another. Each of them loved Jesus and were loved by Jesus. The questions hanging in the air that evening was: Would that love for and from Jesus change the way they loved each other? Would they become a unified family in Christ? Or, would they settle for isolated expressions of faith?

This same command and question hangs over your community: Will the love that each of you have received from Christ spill over into love for one-another?

Jesus doesn't allow for an ambiguous definition of love. He makes clear what it means to love one-another: "There is not greater love than this, than to give one's life for a friend" (Jn. 15:13). We love one-another with the same love God has for us: sacrificial.

Jesus makes clear this is the only way to be a disciple. "This is how everyone will know you are my disciples" (Jn. 13:35). The mark of being a follower of Jesus isn't prayer, meditation, knowledge, or musical tastes: It's love for one-another.

Jesus is emphatic with this implication of the gospel. Anyone who receives the love of God, loves their fellow disciple. He repeats the command over and over through the evening. We love God and love one another because Christ loved us.

Missional Communities are actively growing in their love for one-another. A missional community is a family more than it is a team. We live the gospel by loving one-another. This is biblical community.

LEARNING TO ENTER COMMUNITY

In our culture we call a group of people that care for one-another community. Broken families, codependent relationships, and an epidemic of loneliness have created a ravenous hunger for "community" in this generation. This is what we long for in and outside of the church. Community has become something we consume to meet our needs, not an act of loving others.

Our desire and attempts at filling our needs *through* community has clouded our understanding of what community is. To understand what true community is we must clear the deck of all the things community isn't, or rather, the way we attempt to consume community.

Missional Community Isn't[2]:

- A Social Club—centered on your relational and social needs.
- A Counseling Group—centered on your emotional needs.
- A Social Service Group—centered on your need to change the world.
- A Neighborhood Association—centered on your neighborhood.
- An Affinity Group—centered on your stage of life and preferences.
- An Event or Meeting—centered on a convenient time-slot.

To enter into true community, our desire to use community to meet our needs must be surrendered. Community cannot meet the needs you are seeking to gain from it. Turn those desires to God instead of community. Dietrich Bonhoeffer clarifies this well:

> *"Christian brotherhood is not an ideal which we must realize; it is rather a reality created by God in Christ in which we may participate."*

GROWING IN OUR LOVE AS FAMILY

The dominate metaphor for Christian community throughout the New Testament is family. God is father: We are adopted by him through Christ, we are brothers and sisters, we are heirs, and we have received every spiritual blessing. From Abraham onward, God's purposes of blessing and salvation are worked out through a family. From Jesus' death and resurrection onward, the Church becomes a diverse family belonging to a community and belonging to God. The family of God is

---

2 This is a modified list based on teachings that were helpful from Soma. www.wearesoma.com

characterized by the Father, who is loving, compassionate, gracious, merciful, patient, and just. Those who have been adopted into salvation are no longer orphans because of sin, but belong because of God's love.

It is from this place of experience and knowledge of divine love that anyone is able to love others within community. We receive grace, so that we can extend grace to our brothers in Christ. It is from knowing God's patience and mercy, that we live patiently and mercifully with our family. Christian community is authentic, generous, and caring because God is truth, grace, and love.

This sort of family is not an ideal we have to realize, but rather a reality created by God in Christ in which we participate. Instead of finding our motivation in our own prescribed needs and desires, we cling to loving one other because we have received God's love. Christian community is one of consistent and mutual extension of grace, truth, faith, hope, and love not for the sake of receiving it but from the joy of giving.

GROWING IN LOVE BY GIVING YOURSELF

Within this familial community, each of the "one another commands" makes sense:
- Comfort one another (2 Cor. 13:11)
- Agree with one another (2 Cor. 13:11)
- Live in peace with one another (2 Cor. 13:11)
- Greet one another (2 Cor. 13:11)
- Bear one another's burdens—which in context refers to confronting sin and being burdened for the sinful brother (Gal. 6:2)
- Bear with one another (Eph. 4:2)
- Encourage one another (1 Thess. 5:11)
- Build one another up (1 Thess. 5:11)
- Do not grumble against one another (James 5:9)
- Do not speak evil against one another (James 4:11)

Through these "one-another's" we become family in experience. These command are the process and action toward an authentic life of community where people care for one another. They are also commands that say unequivocally that community is a place of giving of your self.

Being a member of God's family requires death to self. You must die. Community is costly. As the Apostle Paul write in Colossians 3:9, put off the old self:

Do not lie to one another, seeing that you have put off the old self with its practices and have put on the new self, which is being renewed in knowledge after the image of its creator. Here there is not Greek and Jew, circumcised and uncircumcised, barbarian, Scythian, slave, free; but Christ is all, and in all. — Colossians 3:9-11

Here Paul is telling us exactly the way toward familial community: become new through God and be formed in the image of God. Now, all of this sounds very utopian and pleasant. Who wouldn't want to be "fixed" and experience a caring and authentic community where your burdens are carried, you are not alone, and you are known? We all would, but a community like this is costly. It requires a death to you. It requires leaving your identity in yourself—what you do, what you have, where you came from.

In the place of this dying self, you will cling to the new self which is being formed by God and is in the image of God. They way toward an authentic community is God recreating us. In Christ, we are not known by our culture, ethnicity, status, or resources. Those labels do not fit within a missional community, because we are all defined by Christ. He is recreating every aspect of our hearts.

Paul, then, goes on to describe the cost and fruit of this new identity in Christ:

"Put on then, as God's chosen ones, holy and beloved, compassionate hearts, kindness, humility, meekness, and patience, bearing with one another and, if one has a complaint against another, forgiving each other; as the Lord has forgiven you, so you also must forgive. And above all these put on love, which binds everything together in perfect harmony. And let the peace of Christ rule in your hearts, to which indeed you were called in one body. And be thankful. Let the word of Christ dwell in you richly, teaching and

admonishing one another in all wisdom, singing psalms and hymns and spiritual songs, with thankfulness in your hearts to God. And whatever you do, in word or deed, do everything in the name of the Lord Jesus, giving thanks to God the Father through him." — *Colossians 3:12-17*

We exchange our self-interested, self-defined, and approval seeking lives for one where we know we are approved of and chosen by God. The new life is one in community where we live with pure and loved hearts. Now we clothe our lives with kindness and humility! This is how we bear with one another, how we forgive one another: by being made new by God, by receiving new hearts of compassion.

Paul then points to key pillar of community: forgiveness. You will not hold grudges, judge others, snicker behind others' backs, figure our what their problem is and hold it over them, or force them to earn your acceptance through right living. No, you don't get to do any of those things and you don't want to. Instead you forgive.

How can you forgive? You have been forgiven. Or, in other words, you received compassion from God who did not snicker at you or make you earn his approval. With a first hand knowledge of being accepted, welcomed, and forgiven, you extend it to others. This will stretch you.

The pattern of life in this world is to use others' mistakes, errors, and missteps against them and for you. Our sins define us and their sins define them. However, in Christ, we are defined by the love God poured out on us to forgive us our sins. We are defined by that love. This love rules in community. This love overcomes burdens. This truth brings peace amidst all kinds of suffering. This grace produces thankful hearts. This is the love of Jesus. Paul says that this love rules community (1 Cor. 13).

You could sum up all of the one-another commands in the New Testament into this one: love one another. But what kind of love? The greatest kind of love: self-donating and self-giving love. The love exemplified by Jesus on the cross, where he gave his life: body, presence, and future. On the cross we see the love that is required within his community. We see on the cross the commandment lived out. Jesus doesn't ask us to live out an ideal for our sake, or require us to do something he will not do. Jesus is calling us to be conformed into the image of the Creator. To be like Jesus is to love like he loved and to extend that love to the ones he chose to love. This is why we love one another. What are the implications of letting this love rule our hearts as we live alongside others?

- We don't give from the margins.
- We don't give from convenience.
- We don't give from comfort.
- We don't give our left-overs.
- We don't give from insecurity.

Rather we . . .

- We give ourselves with joy.
- We give ourselves with generosity.
- We give ourselves with truth.
- We give ourselves with humility.
- We give ourselves with forgiveness.
- We give ourselves with confidence, not allowing our community to live in sin, worship idols, and disregard Jesus as savior.
- We give because God gave Christ.
- We love because Christ loved us.

This is the type of familial community our souls actually crave. This is the only expectation big enough for lasting community.

THE IDEAL: GROWING IN DEVOTION AND UNITY

This is what happens in the book of Acts after the people had heard the gospel preached by Peter and responded to it in repentance and belief. After they received the gospel they changed the way they lived together:

> "And they devoted themselves to the apostles' teaching and the fellowship, to the breaking of bread and the prayers. And awe came upon every soul, and many wonders and signs were being done through the apostles. And all who believed were together and had all things in common. And they were selling

their possessions and belongings and distributing the proceeds to all, as any had need. And day by day, attending the temple together and breaking bread in their homes, they received their food with glad and generous hearts, praising God and having favor with all the people. And the Lord added to their number day by day those who were being saved." — Acts 2:42-47

The two key words in this passage are "devotion" and "together." Devotion means to persist with closely or serve personally. Or in other words, attach yourself to the service of another. Here we see a glimpse of the early church, a community of people who were devoted not only to Jesus but also to one another. We see a beautiful picture of the results of a community of people who were so devoted to the gospel that they were devoted to one another. There isn't even a taste of self-focused consuming of relationships or the desperate seeking of fulfillment from others. Instead, they were a people secure in God's grace and salvation who engaged community as people full and ready to give.

Connected to this devotion is their togetherness or their finding all things in common—unity. Their devotion to Jesus and one another resulted in unity. They lived more like a tight family than a loose collection of individuals. They didn't consume each other. They clung to the gospel. You don't get unity by being nice, tolerant, or experts in conflict resolution strategies. Paul describes the cause of our unity in Ephesians 4:1-6:

"I therefore, a prisoner for the Lord, urge you to walk in a manner worthy of the calling to which you have been called, with all humility and gentleness, with patience, bearing with one another in love, eager to maintain the unity of the Spirit in the bond of peace. There is one body and one Spirit—just as you were called to the one hope that belongs to your call— one Lord, one faith, one baptism, one God and Father of all, who is over all and through all and in all."

Paul connects his charge for their unity, love, caring, and patience to their common Lord. Paul says, you are one (unified) because you have one Lord, one faith, one baptism, and one God. You achieve unity not through rules of engagement but through a shared ruler over all life. We live as family because we all belong to "one God and Father." This is why we are eager to maintain unity.

The church in Acts 2 expresses their devotion and unity in activity. Community is not simply an idea we think about but requires action and obedience. This community prayed together and they ate together. They shared the gospel teachings, and they shared their possessions to meet needs! They welcomed others into their homes and they received from one another with generous hearts. They did not live in a holy huddle or commune, but they did share moments of life in meals and in their homes. More importantly, they shared the struggles of life and the joys of life. Therefore the ideal community is one growing in devotion and unity. This the biblical pattern.

STEPPING INTO A COMMUNAL LIFE

What if we tried to recover this biblical pattern of community? What if we decided not to be a group of individuals who try to follow Jesus on our own, occasionally gathering for a church service or a bible study; rather, we committed to being a community of people devoted to Jesus and one another! What if we decided not to use community but tried to be faithful to Jesus through community?

This type of community is terrifying. It's one thing to have a relationship with someone centered on a hobby or an event but to have it centered on the gospel is entirely different. Many people jump into community hoping it will meet their needs. If you've turned to community for healing, significance, or acceptance, you've probably been burned. We fear community won't "work" even after putting in all the effort. What if I fail the community before it fails me?

The hope of the gospel is that we don't have to be a perfect community since Jesus was perfect for us. When we let one another down, we point to Jesus who lifts us up. The gospel, not religious rules, unites the church. Religious community, however, says: "If I keep the community rules, then people will accept me," but gospel community says: "We are already accepted in Christ; therefore, we love, forgive, and accept one another." This is great news! The gospel frees us from performing for God or for the church! You don't have to impress God because Jesus impressed God for you. You don't have to pretend to be perfect because all of us are imperfect people clinging to a perfect Christ, being perfected by the Spirit!

HOW TO GROW IN DEVOTION AND UNITY
Spend Time Together

We certainly can't be family growing in our love for one-another if we settle for just being together once a week, but we also live busy lives with many commitments. We have a lot going on with our jobs, school, families, hobbies, and the ordinary demands of everyday life (laundry, cleaning, cooking).

Remember, church isn't something you attend; it's something that you are! You are the church as you work, go to school, participate in sports, enjoy hobbies, and do ordinary things. Do ordinary things but with gospel intentionality. In other words, do the everyday things of life but do them in a way that shows your devotion to Jesus, one another, and your neighbors and city! We encourage one another to do things you already do but to do them with others in community.

Think through your average week: *What are some of your commitments and weekly rhythms?* Here's a list to get you started.

- Chores/Errands: Yard-work, home improvement, auto care, grocery shopping, etc
- Recreation: Vacations, hobbies, exercise, sports leagues, book clubs, etc.
- Meals: Most people eat twenty-one meals a week. You could share a few of these with people in your community.

Share Stories and Hear Stories

Story is a gateway to the soul. Sharing our stories (the good, bad, ugly, and burdensome) is exposing our souls. It takes a brave person to tell another how they truly feel, where they've truly been, and share their scars. However, if you hope to be an authentic and caring community someone will have to share their story with that sort of courage. You will also have to create a safe environment for that to happen which will require a love in hearing the true stories of others.

Tips on story sharing in community:

- Set-up the time as something substantial and vulnerable. As you establish a culture of authenticity you will want to combat gossip, curiosity for curiosity's sake, and nosiness. You are not sharing stories just to figure out what is "wrong" with everyone but to care for them and know where they are.
- Leaders share first. Leaders get to set the mark on authenticity. If a leader models vulnerability and honesty, others will follow.
- Keep stories short, hitting on what we call the "stars" and "scars" of a person's life, but not having to get into the nitty-gritty details.
- Don't feel like the story needs to end in a nice bow.

After the story, you will want to encourage the listeners to ask questions related to what they shared, but not just to get more information, pray for the person sharing, and bless them with words related to what they shared. When someone shares something honest you thank them for being honest, acknowledge their bravery, and avoid becoming a problem solver. You want to ask the storyteller how you can pray for them then do it.

Finally, you don't want this to be a one-hit wonder, rather you want to continue sharing stories and learning more about each other and not just isolated to "story-time." Encourage the community to share meals with each other and for it to be a regular thing to ask each other how they are doing and follow up on what they share. Note: You cannot care for one another in a time-slot.

Share Needs And Let People Help

Set aside time in your organized community gatherings to ask if anyone needs help, whether it is yard-work, house work, finances, car care, etc. No matter what it is, let people share their needs then help each other. Use whatever skills, talents, or money you have to care for each other's felt needs. Dietrich Bonhoeffer calls this communal activity, "active helpfulness," and that's exactly what it is.

This stuff, over time, will lead to deeper needs being shared. Showing up to weed a yard is actually a good sign you might show up at the hospital to sit and pray. If you notice people who are regular helpers but never the receiver of help, this is a sign they don't see themselves as are part of the community yet. Or, they are carrying burdens they don't think the community can help with. Either way, as a leader this gives you something to pray about and something to ask the person: "I've noticed, you guys never ask for help why is that?"

Suffer Together

There are many needs that we experience where the community is helpless. One of the marks of a community that truly cares for one another is the sharing of burdens that cannot be solved by community—for example, terminal cancer, the loss of a parent or child, mental illness, infertility, job loss. In each of these situations, there are tangible ways in which a gospel family can serve and care for the person suffering. However, it doesn't remove the suffering. You can't serve it away. These are opportunities to come alongside those suffering and join them in it. You simply weep as they weep. You listen as they share. You become physically and spiritually present, without a hint of expectation that you can "fix" anything, except allow the other person to know they are not alone and they are seen, heard, and loved.

This is radical in our culture. We usually hide from the issues we mentioned above, hoping the grieving or hurting person just gets over it quickly. We may be there with meals the first few weeks, but then we don't know what else to say. When you get to the point where you don't know what to say, just be present and suffer alongside them. Don't offer hallmark cards or platitudes, but cry with them and share simple truths about God's character. Don't offer explanations for why terrible things happen, offer yourself as a person who wants to walk through their pain with them and as someone who will point the the pain that Jesus carried on our behalf to make all the sad things untrue.

CHRIST BUILDS COMMUNITY OUT OF THE MESS

Despite all these tools and ideas, you cannot create a community that bears with each other in love. In fact, I can guarantee there will be awkwardness, empty promises, lies, disappointments, and mini disasters. Despite all of your attempts to clarify the gospel and the implication that we ought to love one another, the people you lead will not. Your community, more often than not, will fell like it is only a few steps away from falling apart.

This disappointment often brings out the hero complex in leaders. As they help shape a community and begin to watch people grow in caring for one another, they may be tempted to wrap up each persons' story by themselves. As things go poorly for different members or the whole, they rush to solve things. They force conflict resolution meetings, interventions, and tell people what to do next. When things still go poorly, they blame themselves. All the while they've lost sight of the Christ who called them to community. The Savior who forms in. The God who leads it.

Other leaders approach this disappointment by looking for new recruits. They look at the chaos of their missional community and conclude, "If only I had some serious radical Christians this would work. These people just don't get it." In the words of Eugene Peterson: "There are no green beret Christians." While you covet people who "get it," God has given you a few sorry saints to simply love. Not control and not to dismiss, but to love the way Jesus loved his disciples.

Leaders, don't miss out on the transformative joy of growing in love for your fellow brother or sister. Surrender your ideal of community. When you do, the pressure is off and you find Christ forming his people.

REFLECTION&DISCUSSION

What motivates you to pursue community? What holds your community together? What makes it tick? What forces you to get together and fosters conversations throughout the week? What is the dominant topic of conversation? Why do you exist? We all know the answer is supposed to be Jesus, but what is it real? What is the thing that causes your community to exist, gather, and share life. What forms and binds your community together?

- Is the neighborhood or your geography the center?
- Is the "model" central? What about a leader? Spiritual gifts?
- Is the Bible the center?
- Is sin the center? Or one person's struggle?
- Is a common interest, or stage of life holding you together?
- Is it a meal that you plan? Is it a time each week?
- Is it the gospel?

PREPARATION&PLANNING

- How could your community sacrifice in caring for one another?
- How could your community be a place where people share their crises, heart-ache, and tangible needs without needing to solve them?
- How can your community be a place where grace, mercy, and generosity are extended to those within your community who have need (emotional, relational, physical)? Has anyone ever expressed need in your community?
- What can your community do to both care for the needs of the group and speak the truth to each other out of love and not duty, judgment, or savior complex?

CHAPTER 7 |

MISSION: GROWING IN OUR LOVE FOR THE CITY TOGETHER

"The whole law is fulfilled in one statement: "Love your neighbor as yourself." — Galatians 5:14

"Mission is not ours; mission is God's. Certainly, the mission of God is the prior reality out of which flows any mission that we get involved in. Or, as has been nicely put, it is not so much the case that God has a mission for his church in the world but that God has a church for his mission in the world. Mission was not made for the church; the church was made for mission-God's mission." — Christopher Wright

God's mission is to make all things new: to redeem and restore the world. His mission is for all to hear, know, believe, repent, and be raised to abundant life. In God's grace, he not only comes to save us, but sends us out to participate in this magnificent mission. God sets sin's captives free and they use that freedom to point others to their rescuer. God welcomes orphans into his family as they to invite others into the family. God brings to life those dying from sin, to proclaim the good news of resurrection. God invites us, through the gospel, into this mission. Jesus commands us to love our neighbors and then sends us to towns, villages, and cities.

A missional community is a group of people who are devoted to Jesus, to one another, and to their neighbors and city! They are disciples of Jesus who are committed to making more disciples of Jesus! Therefore, mission is not merely a monthly trip to feed the homeless or a trip to Africa to serve in an orphanage (although those are great things to do!). Mission is a primary and regular expression of gospel-centered community.

HOW DO WE LOVE OUR CITIES TOGETHER?
We Speak and Serve

Jesus sends his disciples on the mission of preaching the gospel and confronting evil. Missional communities speak the gospel to their neighbors and the poor, they will also demonstrate God's grace, justice, and love through their actions. Gospel word and deed is simultaneous, just as Jesus preached the gospel of the kingdom and brought the kingdom as he healed. A community centered on Jesus does not stay safe and secluded from the world but runs toward it or better: it invites others into it.

Your community is called, by Jesus, to make disciples and care for the poor. Which is not two callings but one. As you care for the poor, you invite others to follow Jesus. As you invite people to follow Jesus, you care for the poor. As you invite people to follow Jesus, you invite them to care for the marginalized. As you care for the marginalized, you speak the truth of the gospel. As you invite people to follow Jesus, you bless them with words, actions, and gifts. You show them grace as you speak grace. Participating in God's mission is word and deed; speaking and doing.

We Seek Relationship and Justice

The people you are called to love and disciple will have many needs. There will be service projects, collections, and donations. Emptying your pocket book will likely be part of following Jesus into his mission. Blessings and gifts will be prevalent.

The often forgotten gift and the hardest one to give is the gift of relationship. True care for the marginalized requires relationship with the vulnerable. It is through relationship that someone actually travels from being marginalized to being known. When someone becomes a friend and a member of a community, they are no longer being pushed to the outside of society but are being welcomed into the center of it. Imagine the people you are on mission with sitting at your dinner table, sharing a meal, and sharing stories with you. Imagine receiving new relationships from those you are sent to. The mission is not a project. The mission is people.

WHAT IS YOUR COMMON MISSION?

There is and always has been both an individual and communal aspect to being on Jesus' mission. As you enter the spheres of life God has thrown at you, go as God's messenger, go knowing you are part of a community of messengers that will play a role in your seemingly individual mission.

However, you are called to work together and be together on mission too! Jesus sent his disciples out into villages *together*. The early church sent teams of people into new areas *together*.

Consider how your community shares the mission of making disciples. How can your community focus and unify around making disciples? This isn't an activity but proactive and communal decision to love a specific people.

Remember our definition of a missional community. A missional community is a way to organize the church to gather and send groups of people on a common mission, (i.e. to engage artists in the city, engage a neighborhood, or help the homeless downtown).

A common mission is your community's unified effort to love—through word and deed—a specific group of people. As you set out to start and lead a missional community, one of the first things you have to think about is: what will our common mission be. Three broad categories for common missions exist: geographic, network, and marginalized.

A Neighborhood as Common Mission

This common mission focuses your community to make disciples through word and deed of people who live around you. This mission aims at reaching people who share the same spaces: streets, grocery stores, restaurants, and parks. This can be very dynamic as your community can begin making decisions around where it shops, drinks coffee, and how it interacts with neighbors. Some great next steps include joining the neighborhood association meetings, finding needs within the community to meet, and becoming the people who welcome new people in and create space for people to get to know each other.

Geography can be particularly appealing for a community where the majority of the people live in the same neighborhood, subdivision, apartment complex, or dorm. It is also a good common mission in contexts where people feel a strong sense of neighborhood pride and spend most of their time within a short distance of their homes. Furthermore, it is great because it simply requires a group effort to be intentional through their daily life at home.

Many of our missional communities focus on our neighborhoods. We host block parties, neighborhood art camps, and spend time cleaning and caring for the neighborhood elementary and middle school grounds. We try to seek the welfare of the Hosford/Abernathy neighborhood by keeping up to date with its needs. Through all of this we build relationships and bonds with our neighbors. We invite our neighbors over for dinners, hear their stories, and share the gospel whenever we have opportunity. Many of our missional communities experience a lot of favor too. Neighbors enjoy having people that gather and bond people together. Through this type of mission, many communities begin to care for the needs of single mothers, people with disabilities, and the working poor.

However, geography isn't a good common mission for every community. If the people in your community don't live close to one another, this probably isn't a good common mission. If the majority of the people are commuting into a neighborhood to do "life-on-life" mission, then it is shallow and traction is incredibly difficult to come by. Honestly, it's just kind of weird to have people "reach a neighborhood" they don't live in.

One final caution: if you engage in a geographic centered mission, how will you care for the poor and welcome "the other" into your community? We often find ourselves in neighborhoods that are isolated from the issues of poverty, crime, and injustice. How will your community step into needs, even if you don't find them within your neighborhood?

A Network as Common Mission

How can your community share mission if it doesn't share a neighborhood? Your community can be on mission within the same network of relationships. For example, your missional community could focus and unite around making disciples of artists, musicians, or writers. But it doesn't have to be just within the arts, a community could also unite around a gaming community or an athletic team.

One of our early missional communities focused on a public house that hosted children nights and trivia nights. They jumped into this mission where they built relationships with the pub staff and the regulars (even though many in the community lived far way). They also served this space by helping start an open mic night. This proved to be a great way to step into relationship with those who didn't know Jesus.

This is a great common mission to share if a community has common interests or an already existing network. Some of the challenges with this mission include embracing others and not become an exclusive club and including children.

A People as Common Mission

Who are the vulnerable in your neighborhood, city, or town? The marginalized are those who don't get to experience the full-life of the city. They are overlooked, unheard, isolated, or pushed to the fringes of your city's culture. Every city has neglected children or orphans. Your city has elderly, shut-ins, Alzheimer patients, and retirement homes few visit because our culture views them as past their usefulness and relevance. Your city daily welcomes refugees and immigrants hoping to build a life and experience freedom. Your city is made up of single parents, people struggling with mental illness, teenage runaways, people struggling with substance abuse. These are the people your city uses and ignores—the poor and powerless.

Jesus pursued people because they were created in his image and loved them. These people were welcomed into Jesus' community as his beloved and his disciples. I believe Jesus calls his people to not only meet needs (cloth, visit, and feed) but also welcome into relationship. Jesus healed people and fed them, but the most powerful expressions of his love for them was when he invited them to his dinner table.

One of the big challenges (and big opportunities) with this common mission is the reality that the poor are kept away from many in the church today. Tim Chester describes this reality well in his book *Unreached*:

> *"Friendship evangelism is great, but it does not enable the gospel to travel beyond our social networks, unless there are intentional attempts to build friendships with people who are not like us."*

John Mark Hobbins of London City Mission writes:

> *"Many people live in networks which take precedence over their address, and many churches have grown because of this. But the reality for many people living in social housing or in cheaper housing is that their address is very likely to define their daily life."*

If you were to engage in a life of mission to the marginalized, you would have to plan it, prepare for it, and strategically change your life to create avenues of engagement. All of that just to break through social, economic, and physical geographic barriers and get to a place where you could share life with the oppressed.

Mission to the poor requires a concerted and collective effort towards unlikely friendships and distant neighbors. This is the greatest strength to having a common mission: you have to work at it and do it together. This mission requires a giving of yourself and a loving of the other in your city.

This common mission is also one that welcomes in neighbors, co-workers, and friends. As you meet and engage the people neglected in your city, your city notices. As we serve and engage in relationship with the poor, we get to invite our neighbors into mission as they explore what it means to follow Jesus.

One challenge is the potential of placing yourself and your community as the "hero" and rescuer who swoops in and fixes people's problems. That's not true and it's not good. Another challenge is seeing people as service projects instead of people. The challenges and rewards of this type of common mission are many.

MOVING FORWARD IN MISSION TOGETHER

Every community and mission is unique. The cookie cutter doesn't even exist. However, the best place to start is to listen to the people you are sent to and reflect on how their lives might intersect the gospel and community.

Understand the Mission

Here are five sets of questions to help you move forward in discipling others as a community with the gospel.

1. **People:** Who are the people is God sending us to? Where do they live and hang out? What are their stories? What are their names? What are the avenues to engage and build relationship?
2. **Language:** What "language" do they speak? Are these people young families, business professionals, working class, etc?
3. **Value:** What is most important to them? Success, money, relationships, independence, survival, comfort, escape, etc? Who speaks into their worldview?
4. **Gospel:** What false gospel do they believe in? In other words, what do they hope for? What is the "problem" in their eyes? What is the solution? How is the gospel good news to them? How does it address their values? How is the gospel better than what they value most right now?
5. **Needs:** What are their needs? How does Jesus meet those needs? How can we be part of meeting their needs in a way that "shows" the gospel?

Know What You Have to Offer

What are the gifts, resources, and passions of the community? Who is in your group? What has God given you as a people—not simply possessions, but talents, abilities, hobbies, etc? What is it that you have to offer these people as a community? Likewise, how will your community begin to rely on and expect relationship from those you are sent to?

As you create this list, you will quickly realize you do not have enough. Your community doesn't have what it takes, you don't have the resources to solve homelessness in your city. This is the right place to be. It will push you to prayer and push you to faithfulness in taking steps with humility. Don't be proud of what you have to give, come to mission dependent. Also, don't come defeated. Come with the confidence that Jesus is enough.

Lead Into the What

1. Commit to a new pattern of life. You are going to have to change the way you live to engage in relational ministry with the marginalized. Things will change.
2. Create a plan of patiently speaking and demonstrating the gospel. Planning requires putting things on the calendar, and in the budget. Make a plan together that allows you to do be on mission together. If you don't plan it, it probably won't happen.
3. Once you've planned it, show up. This takes resolve. The planning part of our brain is rational and taps into the deep longings of our souls. The in the moment decision making part of our brain taps into our primal desires for comfort and pleasure. Making a plan is huge but overcoming the urge to call it off or call in sick is also huge.
4. Once you show up, evaluate how it went as a community. Ask questions like, how did it feel? What fears did doing this bring up? Who wanted to show up? What was it that got exposed in your own heart as you served. Also, evaluate the mission: what do we need to grow in to be better missionaries? How do our hearts need to change? What did we learn about their true needs? What was encouraging? Do we need to change our plan and do we need to change our prayers? Finally, what did we learn about Jesus?

MISSIONAL COMMUNITIES ARE ALSO SCATTERED

Mission is done in community. A community shares the load of the mission of making disciples. It takes a group to demonstrate Jesus to others. A community on mission is not one that talks about it one night a week and then sends everyone to "try" in their independent lives. No, the mission is shared and God sends us to be on mission together.

However, missional communities also scatter. Through the circumstances of life, we are sent into some arenas of life alone, where the community does not travel with us: at work, at school, and in our homes. A community can engage in those individual spheres sporadically, but the individual or individual family is the constant and consistent image of God. There is and always has been an individual and communal aspect to mission.

Mission is something that happens in our everyday lives as we follow Jesus. Mission is not merely an activity; it is our identity! Being missional is being yourself. It is making disciples where you live.

Whether you work in a high-rise office-building or in your home caring for your small children, you are sent there by God to be his agent of reconciliation. This is how God is making himself known through his people, by sending them out into the world. God actually places more people in your life than you probably realize.

Everyone has neighbors, co-workers, friends, bartenders, yoga instructors, financial advisors, teachers, classmates, fellow PTA members, and a whole slew of family relationships. In other words, God has sent you toward friends who don't follow Jesus or know the gospel. How do you invite those folks to believe the gospel and become followers of Jesus?

We love our cities in the normal things of life: backyard grill-outs with neighbors, lunch breaks with your co-workers, attending concerts, watching films, play dates, and happy hours. The missional church is not about adding activities to an already busy life; rather, it is a matter of being yourself in the everyday with gospel intentionality.

74

BE A LEADER WHO SENDS

At its core and in the bulk of Scripture, God's mission is worked out through people, families, communities, and tribes who are themselves God's witness to the world, God's invitation to the world, and God's message: redeemed and recreated humanity by God's power, grace, and love. The body of Christ is God's physical representative in your neighborhood, workplace, school, and city. Even as you may enter those places alone, it truly takes a "village" to make a disciple.

> *"To make disciples is to call and equip men and women to be signs and agents of God's justice in all human affairs." —* Lesslie Newbigin

As you send your community into each independent sphere of life, send them as God's messenger. Send them knowing they are part of a community of messengers that will play a role in their seemingly individual efforts. Gather them together for the shared and common missional purpose your community has chosen. The communal mission becomes the training ground and the tip of the spear for how the good news will move through you.

REFLECTION&DISCUSSION

How have you experienced God's kingdom breaking into your life?

How have you been a recipient of God's grand mission of making all things new?

When was a time you were able to participate in God's mission in your family, city, world?

What are the different ways, gifts, opportunities people have to walk with God in mission?

How, as a leader, can you unleash the missionary people in your community?

PREPARATION&PLANNING

Where are you and your community with common mission?

What step do you think you are in: choosing a mission, listening/learning, evaluating what you have to give, stepping into the what?

What type of common mission sticks out to you: neighborhood, network, people? What makes sense with your community and context?

What barriers exist between your community and the common mission? What baby step can you pursue?

How can you communicate encourage, equip, and embolden the people in your community for mission?

What is your next step with mission?

GROWING IN LOVE: OUR STORY OF MISSIONAL COMMUNITY

My wife and I waited for their response. We were somewhat nervous, but mostly relieved. We had just come out of the shadows. Our marriage was in trouble. We were in trouble.

This was the night we told our community how bad it was and that we needed intense marriage counseling. The days leading up to our public confession of mess, were filled with interventions from fellow leaders and a painful conversation in which I ask Mirela: "Have there been good times in our marriage?" She responded: "Some but they don't last long." She had been fighting for my attention for quite some time. Our marriage had endured lots of pain we simply raced past: the loss of a parent, deep financial hardships, the US immigration system, and doing ministry in the core of a city that wanted nothing to do with the church.

The bulk of our married life had been spent leading communities, doing ministry, planting a church, and pretending to have a good marriage. This was our fourth missional community to lead. We had already sent three communities out. I had already led trainings on how to 'do' missional community. This was the moment I finally felt like I belonged to a missional community.

It was the first moment we truly asked something from any community. We needed childcare, we needed funds for counseling, and we desperately needed prayers.

We spent the next year simply participating. We weren't the leaders anymore. Mirela and I have never been the same. That community was never the same either. This honest moment ushered in a sort of caring and loving I had stopped expecting from those I was in "community" with. Looking back I realize that I had finally become a burden and I had become a brother.

We sought the gospel together. Mirela and I shared what we were learning in counseling. People saw our marriage transform right before their eyes. Our community paid for months and months of counseling. They watched our daughter. They regularly asked what was going on. Beyond this, each couple examined their own marriage. Mirela and my learning and growing was theirs, too.

Furthermore, it was in this season that I saw the power of simply pursuing love for God, love for one another, and love for neighbor. Emboldened by counseling and my community, I began to share what God was doing in my life with friends and neighbors. In telling them about my mess crazy things began to happen: neighbors wanted to talk about Jesus more. They wanted to come to our church's worship gatherings. They wanted to hear how we saw God's presence in our mess.

When people ask me if missional communities work, I look back to this story and say, yes: they do. This one was vital in nudging me to love God, love his church, and love my neighbors.

PART 3:

LEADERSHIP IN MISSIONAL COMMUNITY

CHAPTER 8 |

WHAT IS IT LIKE TO BE A MISSIONAL COMMUNITY LEADER

"The best and first thing you must do, is accept your irrelevance..." — Eugene Peterson

Leadership is such a strange thing, especially in the West. The position of leadership is idolized while the role of leadership is neglected.

Many children are pushed to being the "leader" of the pack by their parents for no other reason than holding that position. The ambition of leadership (for those that lead) is prestigious in title only. For example, through much of the electoral process for presidents, governors, and prime-ministers, the principle motivation, it seems, for the candidates is to *be* the president. Not *do, live, or serve* as the president. There is a leadership obsession and drive that not only isn't healthy, it isn't leadership. This is the leadership void.

On the flip side, leadership is also distorted among those who have decided to follow. Leaders are viewed as the problem solvers for every issue you have. Followers view leaders like patrons view their waiters: you can place an order and get served until your order arrives. If your order doesn't arrive promptly and as you ordered, you have the right to send it back or walk out of the restaurant.

Within the context of a community, leaders are viewed as those who provide for our social wellbeing: they make sure everyone is involved, connected, and making friends. Leaders are also supposed to provide biblical counsel, care, and help for marriage, emotional, financial, and even romantic struggles.

Leaders are there to *guarantee* that everyone is growing in following Jesus. Leaders are to provide the right amount of inspiration, drive, and vision to compel us to live radical lives, but not too extreme so that we get tired. Followers consume leaders. Sadly, this is often how people view Jesus as their leader. He is the service provider to fix, help, and aid perceived needs. When leaders comply with this view of leadership, we reinforce this picture of Jesus.

The true picture of Jesus' leadership is as a servant-king. Jesus came to make the truth explicit through his words, stories, and actions. He came to call people to repentance, faith, and abundant life.[3] Jesus allowed talented, rich, and popular people to walk away. He also allowed people he led to make mistakes, misunderstand, and even betray him. Jesus came and poured his life out for others. He came as a servant and a king.

We misunderstand leadership. Leadership ought to be defined as taking initiative for the benefit of others. Christian leadership goes even further to define the "others." Leadership is taking initiative for the benefit of Christ, fellow believer, and neighbor. Christian leadership is profoundly a role of service to Jesus. The only hint of romanticism is that of a lost life at the feet of a worthy king.

The Christian leader desires to faithfully labor so that others might catch a glimpse of the gospel. The people you lead are responsible for their own obedience, faithfulness, and growth. You, as a leader, are responsible for creating an environment where people are confronted with the truth and grace of the gospel, challenged to follow and obey Jesus, and spurred on to take hold of the life of hope, mission, and justice they are called to have.

Three metaphors describe the work of a missional community leader: gardener, model, and catalyst.

---

3 He healed people and fed people. However, he did not allow himself to be consumed as a magician performing tricks.

LEADING AS A GARDENER

Gardeners have quite a bit of work to do to create the best possible opportunity for growth. They have to prepare the soil through tilling and fertilizer; they have to plant seeds, water the seeds, remove weeds regularly that would choke out the plants. They also have to wait and see. Despite the regular care, concern, and even expertise of the gardener, they can't force the plants to grow and become fruitful.

I have one of the most ideal set-ups for gardening. I live in Portland where the soil is deep black and nutritious, the sun comes right over our house for long stretches during the summer, and we buy good starters and seeds. Some seasons we have amazing crops and others seasons they are average. Why? I have no idea. Most of the time it is a mystery to me.

One year our crops were below average and it wasn't a mystery. We planted late and haphazardly (we planted tomatoes in the shade), we rarely weeded, and we didn't mulch around the plants to hold in moisture. We basically planted then forgot about the garden. Life got busy, we traveled, and other things occupied our time. When our tomatoes never really produced, and our zucchinis were sub-par, it wasn't a mystery—it was neglect. The real mystery was that our garden produced anything at all!

Leading a gospel community is like being a gardener. You facilitate gospel growth by creating an environment where growth can happen but you can't make people believe and you can't make people obey. You do the best you can to supply the right food a group of people needs to grow up in the love, grace, and truth of the gospel. However, you can't make people grow— you aren't in charge of the fruit.

It's also like trying to get a toddler to eat their veggies. You can put it on the plate, tell them it is good for them, add spices, and be an example by eating them yourself, but you can't force the kid to swallow. This is what leading a gospel community is like.

As a leader, you point to the gospel, speak the gospel, connect the gospel to people's stories, pray in light of the gospel, and call people to serve as demonstrations of the gospel, but you can't make repentance and faith happen. That is God's wonderful work.

It's the mystery of discipleship—which is why gardening is the perfect metaphor for what you are doing as a leader. The bulk of this book, speaks to the things that create a gospel centered environment where people are confronted with the joy and truth of the gospel as members of a community. We are teaching you how to be a gospel gardener

As you step into leadership, you are committing to the regular cultivation of a community around the gospel. You are praying for and expecting growth to happen. You ought to expect the Spirit to be working in people's lives as you share meals, hear stories, pray, learn from the Scriptures, serve the poor, and share the gospel with friends. You can expect growth, just like the gardener who cares for his garden can expect a crop as he prays for the crop to come. Expect the Spirit to convict and increase faith as people step into more and more obedience.

LEADING AS AN EXAMPLE

The other big piece of leading a gospel community on mission is being an example. Leaders are a picture the community can look at as someone who is believing the gospel and walking in obedience. As a leader, you are inviting people to watch your life and follow you as you follow Jesus. At this point people carry heavy leadership baggage.

Being an example has often been the mark of a leader within the Church. However, the example being displayed is one of perfection. Someone with all the answers, free from sin and harmful vices, has the Bible memorized, and always knows the right thing to do. This, however, is a picture of Jesus, not leaders within a community or church. Instead, the example and model we find within the Bible is that the best leaders are humble, repent of their sins, depend on God, boast in nothing except God's grace in light of their sin, and serve their community. We know leaders make big and small mistakes. We know leaders sin, receive rebuke, repent, and worship God. In the end, they should be bold in speaking the gospel because *they need the gospel.* Leaders are desperate for their gracious Savior.

This is what a leader is called to be an example of: repentance, faith, and belief. That type of repentance, faith, and belief produces confident obedience in action. You will likely become frustrated with your community's involvement and engagement in God's mission. Before you create an ultimatum and kick out the slackers, ask yourself how you are being an example of humble obedience. Invite people to live a life of faith by showing it to them first.

LEADING AS A CATALYST

Lastly, leaders of missional communities are catalysts. They speak up and call God's people to the mission, to community, and, most important of all, to belief in the gospel. As a leader, you care about the mission because God has called you to care about it. This is catalytic.

The leader is not the one who stands and says, "I'm going to do this thing. Can you guys encourage me as I do it?" No, a leader stands and says, "God has called us all to make disciples and be disciples, please join me in that journey. How are we going to do that?"

A leader doesn't do all the tasks or come up with the strategy, structure, and execution alone. Leaders are the ones that light a spark and welcome people into gospel community on mission. A leader welcomes people into the mess of it and works with a community to figure out how they will do it together. They don't have to solve each problem or create each opportunity. Leaders initiate by bringing the problems and opportunities up in conversations.

REFLECTION&DISCUSSION

Who is your favorite leader? Who has had the most leadership influence on your life?

How has leadership been distorted for you?

Which picture of a leader is most attractive to you: gardner, example, or catalyst? Which one is the most challenging or scary?

Why is it so easy to turn to controlling a community instead of praying for the community?

PREPARATION&PLANNING

What is your leadership style? What has been your biggest success and failure as a leader?

What can you do to remind yourself to be a servant of Jesus, not demands of others?

How will you continually turn to Christ as the leader of your community?

CHAPTER 9 |

THE CALLING, QUALIFICATIONS, AND RESPONSIBILITY OF LEADERS

"Jesus sends us to be shepherds, and promises a life in which we increasingly have to stretch out our hands and be led to places where we would rather not go. He asks us to move from a concern for relevance to a life of prayer, from worries about popularity to communal and mutual ministry, and from a leadership built on power to a leadership in which we critically discern where God is leading us and our people." — *Henri Nouwen*

AM I CALLED TO LEAD?

Sometimes, people are led to start a missional community through, what most of us would call, the spectacular. They have a dream, and see seemingly bizarre signs, or hear the voice of God. This does happen. We see it through the Bible. Abraham, Moses, and Paul are the big examples. They were simply walking through life (or running from God), when everything was interrupted and their future was certain. Moses left the burning bush knowing how he would spend the rest of his days: leading God's people into freedom and peace. A blinded Paul made his way to Damascus knowing he would spend his life proclaiming the gospel throughout the known world among the Gentiles. Abraham left Ur following God with the hope of being a father to a family that would bless the whole world. The key word for this kind of spectacular call is *sometimes*. A burning bush is not a "calling" requirement.

There are three more "typical" ways God calls people into leadership.

Called to be Reach People with the Gospel

Many times, people cannot help but start a missional community because of the burden for a people to hear and experience the gospel. After months or years of not being able to imagine anything else, they begin to invite others to into a community on mission to the people they are called to. We have seen this happen regularly:

- A couple has several friends and neighbors who want to explore the gospel further, and so the couple forms a community for them to encounter the gospel in community.
- A person is so moved to share the gospel—through word and deed—to women at-risk or coming out of sex trafficking, that they invite others to start a missional community to do that together.
- Several families are so compelled to be a picture of the gospel in their neighborhood they leave their missional community to start a new one with and for their neighbors.

Called to Shepherd People in the Gospel

Similarly, many leaders start and lead missional communities out of a conviction to help others grow. They simply have a burden to see their friends complete in Christ, walking in their identity and understanding the gospel fully. These leaders take up the call for leadership out of an "oughtness" to care and lead others into spiritual health.

Called Out of Necessity: Someone Must Lead

Lastly, people find themselves leading because they are natural servant-leaders. We've seen this happen often. As a missional community multiplies or as the current leaders experience major life-change, a leadership void exists requiring someone to step into it. What we regularly find, however, is those new leaders grow in their calling and conviction as time goes. They continue to a lead a missional community out of a love for the mission *and* the community.

AM I QUALIFIED TO LEAD?

In our years of starting, multiplying, and leading gospel communities in Portland, we have seen this list as the prerequisite for being a good gospel community leader. People who possess these qualities lead their own lives and communities well.

Motivated by the Gospel&Growing in the Gospel

It seems like a given, but many leaders can lead for other reasons. You will be calling people to follow Jesus, not a model, method, or social club. Jesus is your reward, not significance. Being transformed by Jesus is your motivation. To be motivated by the gospel, you have to be receiving the gospel into your life through reading, prayer, community, and struggle.

Desire to Help Others Grow in Faith&Obedience

To lead a gospel community you have to have a desire to help others pursue their belief and their faithfulness. As a leader, you want to be an aid in people's spiritual formation. This is the goal. If you have another goal, you might not be qualified to be a leader.

Commitment to the Long Process

It will take time and will not feel great or exciting most of the time. Longevity is a substantial element to successful community that is growing the gospel. A leader must be invested in the marathon of making disciples. A leader must be prepared to run the race with endurance and live in the urgency of the Spirit, not in our culture. This means speaking the gospel regularly; this means inviting people into the mission regularly; this means clarifying the truth and obedience. This also looks like calling people to repent. A qualified leader will do this without expectation for immediate results but instead with an expectation for God's movement and work.

Prayerful in dependence on the Spirit

The Holy Spirit dwells within you. It is your helper that empowers you to love others. The Spirit reminds you of the gospel, calls you to repentance, and gives your power over sin. Leaders are those who pray and listen to the Spirit. The primary and initial thing all good leaders do is pray for the people they lead.

Have a Servant-Posture

You are a servant to God. You are not building your resume or gaining God's approval by leading a community. Instead, you are selflessly serving. This doesn't mean you are a spiritual-service provider to your group. It simply means you lead with humility. You take initiative for others growth in the gospel. I love this short saying I got from Andrew Picha: "If serving is beneath you, then leading is above you."

Honest with Their Own Mess

Leaders who are honest and open about their struggles to believe the gospel and their struggles in daily life facilitate true community. The leaders struggle when they hide their mess by pretending and keeping up appearances. Good leaders of missional communities confess their doubts and difficulties in following Jesus. This is how they model genuine worship of Christ and invite and equip others to do the same.

Understand They Can't Make People Change

People are transformed by Christ, not you or a model. What you can do as a leader is invite people to come and drink of the gospel. You can make it compelling, clear, and connected to their present life. However, no one can orchestrate change in people's lives. Good leaders know this, trust in it, and respond by praying for their people to taste and see the goodness of God and walk in faithfulness.

Not the Answer Man or Woman

These communities take initiative for their own learning. When there isn't an answer man, they turn to the Scriptures and discover answers together. Leaders have to be confident enough in who they are in Christ to say, "I don't know." If you are driven to always know the answer or come up with an answer on the spot, you probably aren't ready for leadership. As Henri Nouwen writes eloquently in his leadership book, *In the Name of Jesus*:

> *"Christian leaders cannot simply be persons who have well-informed opinions about the burning issues of our time. Their leadership must be rooted in the permanent, intimate relationship with the incarnate Word, Jesus, and they need to find there the source for their words, advice, and guidance."*

WHAT IS MY RESPONSIBILITY AS A LEADER?

As a leader, you will point people to the gospel in the Bible, speak the gospel in your own words, connect the gospel to people's stories, pray in light of the gospel, and call people to serve as demonstrations of the gospel. Leaders create an environment where community can happen. Here are the primary expectations:

- Prayer for individuals in your community.
- Regularly ask how your people are doing as individuals and families? How are you all doing together? What conversations do we need to have as a community
- Regularly think about your communities journey through the lens of repentance and faith.
  - How is God's kindness leading us into repentance?
  - What does obedience look like for us?
  - What is God calling us to?
  - What scriptures do we need to be reading?
  - What times of prayer do we need to have?
  - What spiritual disciplines do we need to engage?

- Help your community grow in demonstrating and speaking the gospel in the city. Help members understand and grow in participating in God's mission together and separately.
- Help your community grow in love for God, love for one another, and love for city. This is likely done by initiating conversations about these things and pursuing next steps. Also, this may look like making a Missional Community Commitment (I discuss what this looks like in the final chapter and offer an example in the appendixes). The leader is the one that regularly brings out the Commitment and says: "How are we doing, what do we need to do?"
- Delegate tasks and next steps. If you aren't in charge of everything, you'll need to put others in charge of small things. As a leader, you don't have to make the meals, host, lead discussions, etc. You have to ask other people to do that. (More on sharing leadership in the next chapter).

REFLECTION&DISCUSSION

How would you describe your calling as a leader? What motivates you to lead?

Look over the qualifications, which ones are you certain you meet and which ones are you certain you don't?

What would belief and growth in the gospel look like in these areas?

Prayer for the community may be the most difficult responsibility for MC leaders. Why do you think that is? What changes when leaders pray for their community? How will you plan to pray

PREPARATION&PLANNING

Put Yourself Through a Leadership Assessment

- Spend time praying and looking over the MC Leader's Role Description in the appendix.
- Fill out the assessment checklist (in appendix), first privately, then with your spouse or close friend.
- Invite the leaders in your church to speak into your leadership, spiritual health, and vision for leading a missional community.
- If you're going through this field-guide with a cohort or group, you can assess one another. Look for strengths and weaknesses. Celebrate how the gospel is bearing fruit in each others' lives.

CHAPTER 10 |

SHARING THE LOAD OF A MISSIONAL COMMUNITY

You cannot lead a missional community on your own and you aren't supposed to try. But working with others is hard, especially when you don't know the different roles. This chapter examines the types of leadership roles to be shared and the servant responsibilities to be delegated.

SHARING LEADERSHIP ROLES

Missional Leaders

They lead the community in its common mission. The missional leader is the champion for the mission by reminding the group about the it and why. This leader's role is regularly connecting the group to the mission and letting people know the next steps and opportunities. They are also thinking through the gifts and hearts of each person in their community as they invite them into the common mission. These leaders facilitate the conversations about participating in God's mission and serve as a voice clarifying what mission is and are thinking through how they can create a missional discipleship environment.

Shepherding Leaders

These leaders focus on the internal care of the community. They are thinking through the spiritual formation and discipleship of the people in their community. This person facilitates conversations about growing in our devotion to God and one another. They serve as the voice clarifying what loving Jesus and his community looks like. They regularly ask, "How are we doing loving one another? How are doing at learning to follow Jesus together?"

For the group to explore faith and obedience together, you will need a leader who can guide and lead discussions around the gospel, community, and mission. This leader enjoys teaching and explaining new truths as much as helping others engage those truths with questions. They will be good teachers and good listeners, too. Their job isn't to preach but to help others grow in their understanding of the gospel.

All missional community leaders are called to pray for the people in their community and their gospel growth. All leaders are called to take initiative in the discipleship of others. And, all leaders are called to the mission. The missional and shepherding leaders work together to create the discipleship environment from their unique perspectives. Sharing leadership in this way usually requires monthly meetings to pray, discuss the group, and make a modest plan.

SHARED RESPONSIBILITIES WITHIN A MISSIONAL COMMUNITY

Missional communities require a team effort. Typically, we view the leaders of our community group as the ones who serve, host, lead discussions, and create the environment for *us* to grow. However, any sustainable community that is on mission and sharing life will require a team of leaders.

Sharing responsibilities requires people to operate in their gifts to serve and create an environment of gospel growth. This results in *everyone* in the community having a crucial part to play and submitting to one another in each role. Missional community meals will frequently look more like a leadership team meeting than top down teaching.

Healthy communities share the load of being a community. There are four important servant roles, in addition to the leadership roles mentioned above, that ought to be filled by *different* people. There are others, but these are the important ones to get started.

Meal Planner

You will want to delegate someone who likes to communicate clearly what the plan is for the upcoming week with the food and any other things coming up. Have this person communicate in whatever way is best for everyone (text, email, Facebook), about what to bring for the next meal, parties, service opportunities, etc. This person needs to enjoy communicating, organizing, and delegating.

Prayer Person

This person is responsible for calling the community to prayer. They lead prayer times and are the spokespeople for turning the missional communities attention to asking God and listening to God. and share its prayer requests.

Host

Who can host the weekly meals? Who is blessed by having people in their homes and will think through creating a space that is conducive to sharing an intentional meal and discussion each week? The host ought to be a welcoming person who views their home as an outpost of the kingdom and space to share in gospel conversation.

Being the host doesn't mean they clean up by themselves. From the very first meeting, invite everyone to pitch in with cleaning up after the kids, washing dishes, taking out the trash, and putting the home back the way it was when everyone arrived. Everyone participates in family chores! If your community treats the host family like a restaurant or catering service, you aren't cultivating community.

Children's Coordinator

If your missional community has young kids, you will want to have this servant role. Who can organize the group to care for kiddos during the weekly discussions? This is usually as simple as someone making a calendar and having everyone sign-up. One simple method for structuring the kid's time is to have the adult leaders:

- Teach the kids how to do something the leader is really good at (like play music, soccer, paint, cook, jump rope, etc.). It could be anything.
- Share with the kids an important part of their story in learning who Jesus is and what he has done for them.
- Share their favorite Bible verse and explain what it means and how it has affected their lives.

REFLECTION&DISCUSSION

What pictures of shared leadership can you think of in the Bible? What is good, bad, and ugly about sharing leadership?

Do you have a tendency to try and "do everything" or "tell others what to do?" How will that affect the way you share the load of being a missional community?

Pray for co-leaders and for God to connect you with others who have a similar passion.

PREPARATION&PLANNING

What type of leader are you: missional or shepherding? How will you live out that role distinction?

Who will you share leadership with? What is their leadership like?

How will sharing leadership challenge and grow you in the gospel?

As you envision your community, what responsibilities need to be delegated? What roles are and aren't filled?

SENDING AND LEADING: KORY AND EMILY'S STORY OF MISSIONAL COMMUNITY

Kory and Emily joined our first missional community six years ago. They're story was remarkable: they had lived overseas, experienced mission in Asia, served in churches, and received degrees in theology. Yet, they come to our community frustrated, bitter, and simply confused about disconnect of their beliefs in Christ and their experiences in Christian community. "Church" had chewed them up and spit them out. Years later I realized much of our ministry in Portland was to "re-evangelize" Christians who had forgotten the gospel under the pile of junk, scars, and mishaps of past experiences.

Kory was especially wounded from years of betrayal and abuse in the church. And yet, they couldn't give up on it. We were blessed to give them a space to reengage the community and rediscover the gospel. After a year, they began dreaming of a missional community in their neighborhood. One that would display the gospel and the rich family the gospel creates. They weren't sure if they were ready. In fact, they were positive they weren't ready.

Then one evening, Kory began to share, in front of our entire community, how he hadn't trusted God with their finances. He was scared to trust God. They had experienced difficult times and they withheld generous and thankful giving to others. He wanted to confess, share how God had convicted him, and proclaim God's grace through it all. It was in that moment I knew he was ready to lead a community. It wasn't the books, the degrees, or

their missional expertise that qualified them: it was their ability to receive the gospel in the everyday stuff of life and how they modeled a life of repentance and faith.

The community they started has gone on to foster children, host homeless teenagers, care for a family through a difficult separation, and many other visible signs of fruit. More than anything, from a distance, I've seen them grow in faith and patience.

PART 4:

STARTING AND LEADING
MISSIONAL COMMUNITIES

CHAPTER 11 |

PREPARING TO LAUNCH

Every missional community has three essential ingredients: qualified and called leaders, a clear mission, and a committed core. This is where you must begin as a leader. While everything might not be perfectly clear before you begin (it never is), you will want to have a a an initial plan of action.

A SHARED LEADERSHIP TEAM
Here are just a few diagnostic questions to ask as you launch your missional community:
- Who are the missional co-leaders?
- Who are the shepherding co-leaders?
- Who will host?
- Who will coordinate meals?

A COMMON MISSION
We discussed this crucial element in a previous chapter as well. A common mission is your community's unified effort to love—through word and deed—a specific group of people (neighborhood, network, or people group).
- What is the common mission you will invite others join you in?
- How will your community begin to learn, engage, and share this mission?
- What is the first "baby" step your new community will do on mission together?

A COMMITTED CORE

Pray for the people God will bring into your community. Pray for people to come alongside you and help. Pray for God to bring names to mind. Think through the specific people in your life you want to join your new missional community. They'll need to live or work fairly close to you since it's hard to commute to community. You aren't looking for "all-stars" or elite Christians—they don't exist. Pray for people who will commit to the process of becoming a community. Pray for teachable, humble, and honest people. Pray for people that believe in Jesus!

Before you begin sending invitations and making phone calls, be able to put your hopes and prayers for this new community into words. You need to know why.

- What is a missional community? Why start one? Why this mission?
- What do you hope this will look like in your city and town?
- What are you asking people to commit to?

As you invite people, give them a picture of gospel-shaped community alive in God's mission. As you describe what you are prayerfully starting, avoid making your invitation tailor-made to each person, where you sacrifice your convictions. For example, you really want your friends who are struggling in marriage to join, so you tell them it will be a group that fixes marriages. Invite people into a community that isn't centered on their needs, hobbies, or passions but the gospel of Jesus and his mission.

TIP: Set a Date and Get Started

You have a vision, a name, and a team. The logistics are working out. Now it's time to set a date for your gatherings and get started. Oddly, this can be one of the more challenging steps in the process. You have to overcome the inertia of fear, anxiety, and spiritual warfare to set a launch day.

TIP: Give Your Missional Community a Name

It doesn't have to be creative like a garage band, or spiritual, or from the Bible. However, your missional community needs a name or the default will be "Your Leader's Name Missional Community." This unfortunately reinforces the idea that the community belongs to the leader, that it's their thing, and not *our* priority.

Instead, set the tone from the very beginning by naming community together so it's everyone's community. To be sure, leadership is important and requires an increased level of responsibility, planning, and vision, but healthy communities are ones that get described as "our missional community." Some easy options are naming it after the neighborhood, sub-division, or even the street that will be the focal point for your missional community.

REFLECTION&DISCUSSION

This chapter focuses on the final steps before beginning a community, what are your fears and concerns? What are the prayers (not about logistics) but about the gospel coming to and through your community?

PREPARATION&PLANNING

Using the questions in this chapter or the "Checklist" in the appendix, create a plan of action for launching your missional community down to the very fine details.

Map out leadership, those you will invite into the core, and the logistics.

CHAPTER 12 |

LAYING A FOUNDATION

The early days and weeks of your missional community are very important. Your first task is laying a biblical foundation for missional community.

Spend the first chunk of your time as a missional community growing in biblical understanding of what the gospel, community, and mission are. You can not move forward without laying this foundation. However, your community's foundation will be the composite assumptions and ideals of each individual member. It is painfully difficult to lead a community that doesn't have a biblical foundation on the essentials. I don't recommend trying!

You can lay a biblical foundation in a few ways:
- Study a book of the Bible by asking these questions: what does this teach us about who God is, what he has done, who we are, and how we ought to live in our city? I would recommend Ephesians, Colossians, or 1 Peter. Reading the Bible together with these questions helps a group of people see the connections between the gospel, community, mission while developing an understanding of the Scriptures.
- Use a Missional Community primer or curriculum. There are several options out there by the various missional community tribes. Jonathan Dodson and I have put together an eight-week guide to help communities get started called, *Called Together*. This guide covers the biblical and theological framework for the gospel, community, and mission in a discussion format. *Called Together* also provides simple next steps and weekly plans for the first eight weeks.

BEGIN SHAPING YOUR LIFE IN COMMUNITY

As you begin teaching and shaping your times together in the gospel, you will also want to take baby steps into community. To do this, you have to spend time together and get to know one another's lives. Create space where your community can share experiences. This can be as simple as a picnic or a party. Begin inviting people in your community to share life outside of the scheduled times, too. As a leader, you can lead by asking for help when you do big home projects, or simply welcoming others into activities you are already doing. These are baby steps, but there's never a better time to take them than when your community is in its infancy.

BEGIN SHAPING YOUR LIFE ON MISSION

What is a missional community without a mission? If your community begins with a clear common mission, begin in the very first weeks engaging that mission, even if it is to gather to pray specifically for it or grow in your awareness of it. If you don't begin on mission, it will be difficult to continue and grow into mission.

If your community is not yet on decided on a common mission, carve times out during the week for people to serve the neighborhood your community is in. This can be as basic as picking up trash or as complex as joining a community service event. However, if your hope is for you community to grow in love for others it is best to start your community by engaging your city or neighborhood.

PREPARATION&PLANNING

How will you and your co-leaders lay a foundation on the gospel? Which resource will you use? Who will lead those discussion? What will your "non-formal" times look like in the early days?

Plan the first 8-10 weeks of your missional community with the help of a primer or guide. Include times for the community to grow in its relational connection and engagement on mission.

CHAPTER 13 |

MAKING AND KEEPING
MISSIONAL COMMITMENTS

After laying the foundation of the gospel, the easiest way to continue moving forward is to create a missional commitment or what some call a covenant. This commitment is to God, one another, and your city. Essentially, the group decides together how they will be and grow as a missional community.

The purpose of this book is to help leaders move from theory to practice, from the classroom to the city, and from talking about missional community to being a missional community. James says it this way, "Be doers of the word, not hearers only" (Jas. 1:22).

You might be convinced, at this point, that missional communities are the way to be the church, to really be devoted to Jesus, one another, and our neighbors and city. You probably also realize that won't come easy.

If your community "hears" about missional community but doesn't "do" missional community, with a clear sense of how it applies to your everyday lives, you"ll be like the person who looks in the mirror but forgets who he or she is. This is why I encourage leaders and communities to create covenants. I want you and others to be "blessed in your doing."

THE COMMITMENT
A missional commitment has five sections:
1. How will we grow in our love for Christ?
2. How will we grow in our love for one-another?
3. How will we grow in our love for our city and neighbor?

4. How will we count the cost of being a Missional Community?
5. Signatures and commitment to the gospel and process

By God's Grace We Will Grow in Our Devotion to Christ by . . .

In this first section, you want to come up with ways you will practically grow in your devotion to Jesus this year.

Some groups may commit to reading the Gospels together, attending Sunday gatherings to hear the gospel, discussing sermons over a meal on a weeknight, starting fight clubs, or initiating one-on-one discipleship times. Others may commit to developing their prayer life, memorizing Scripture, attending a conference together, or reading books on gospel marriage or parenting.

This section may include a commitment to Christ-centered study of the Scriptures, sermon discussions, memorizing Scripture together, inviting counsel from the community on a whole range of personal issues, and much more. You may want to cultivate better listening skills in Spirit-led decision-making or devoting entire nights to prayer for one another and the city.

The idea is that you, as a community, answer these questions yourself. Be honest about where you need to grow in your devotion to Jesus this year and be creative and faithful with how you plan to do that. Get honest and get specific!

By God's Grace We Will Grow in Our Devotion to One Another by . . .

This should be fun as you look around at one another and ask: "How would we treat one another differently if we are family?" Since you are family in Christ, why not live like it?!

In this section you may commit to share more meals or help each other out. For example, help one another in employment search, financially, with childcare, with transportation, and the list goes on and on.

You may also include a commitment to sharing more of your lives by getting to know each others' stories and spending time together.

This is exciting because no two groups are the same. Your community can be devoted to one another in unique ways. This is where you get to commit to those things!

By God's Grace We Will Grow in Our Devotion to Our Neighbors and City by . . .

Here is where you get to think like a missionary. You get to look around, pray and ask God to show you who he is calling you to make disciples of.

Don't just stop at identifying your mission, but get specific on a plan to engage the mission. How can you orient your lives to spend time with the people you are called to? How is the gospel good news to those people?

Try to get specific, realizing that the Lord is also sending everyone into individual missions throughout the city. Take time to recognize the mission field of vocation and discuss how you can support one another in that. However, don't just state a generic mission. We have found that the broader the mission, the less traction it gets.

We Will Count the Cost of Being a Missional Community by . . .

Following Jesus will cost you something and that is actually good news in the Kingdom of God as it is more blessed to give than receive! I often see, as a result of God's grace, everyday people begin to be radically generous with their time, their creativity, and their finances.

It is important to "count the cost" in making a Missional Commitment and to get specific on how you plan to give. Some good questions to ask are:
- How can I be generous with my time?
- How can I be generous with my creativity?

- How can I be generous financially to see the gospel go forward in our community, our church, our city, and beyond!

By God's Grace, We Commit to the Process of Becoming a Missional Community

Since Jesus Christ is the head of the church and the center of your community, he should be your primary focus. Every issue in the lives of the community has an answer in Christ. As a community, you have the wonderful privilege of joining together to explore, through the ups and downs, how Christ is central and meaningful.

In this section you are committing to being a community that "speaks the truth in love" to one another. You are committing to be a confessing, counseling, repenting community, which continually reorients one another to Christ and his promises.

This section only needs to be a simple affirmation of the gospel in your own words and how any success with be God's grace.

DISCLAIMERS ON USING COMMITMENTS
You Will Fail

You won't perfectly live out what you commit to: you never do. The good news is that when you fail in loving one another and your neighbors, you have the gospel wherein God freely forgives us! You don't "do missional community" to earn Gods favor; rather, in Christ you have God's favor to be a missional community, imperfections and all!

This commitment should not serve as a legalistic document to judge one another's performance; rather, it should be something you can revisit regularly to see how you are progressing in living out your devotion to Jesus, one another, and your neighbors and city.

This is Not an Attempt to Create "In" or "Out"

Some people sit through these discussions but are not ready to make a missional commitment, that's okay. Although you want everyone to be challenged and encouraged to be a faithful disciple of Jesus, you are not here to twist arms. You're glad everyone is here.

In fact, encourage those who don't want to make a commitment to continue being part of your missional community. Let them know: "We want you with us." The Missional Commitment is not intended to create an "in or out" dynamic, but, rather, to clarify a common commitment to being a community that lives out what you believe in everyday life. This commitment will help shape a core of committed people that will benefit your whole community and city.

Be Committed to the Process

Missional community is a mess and a process. A community leaning into this process is the ideal missional community on this side of new creation. A community that engages the journey of being conformed into the image of Christ is a dynamic picture of the gospel the city needs. Your calling is to start where you are and take steps forward, through prayer, study, shared meals, showing up to serve, inviting others in, and becoming increasingly present in your city.

A great missional community is one that regularly asks: how are we allowing the gospel to shape us? What is God calling us to? How is God challenging us to be conformed into the image of Christ? This is the whole deal! Don't get stuck in the details of your commitment but allow them to evolve as God opens doors and new challenges.

MISSIONAL COMMITMENT TIPS:
- This should all fit on two pages max. Any more than that and you're going overboard.
- Be specific and start small. Don't try to plan a take over of the city in your first missional commitment.
- Let your first MC Commitment be for only a semester then reevaluate.

- Let your MC Commitment be your leadership guide. Once it is created, review with the your co-leaders monthly. How can you help your community move forward in one area this month? What do you need to talk or do when you get together? Is your community balanced? What areas of growth need to be celebrated? What areas need to be challenged?

EPILOGUE

Mirela and I began our first missional community in Portland over six years ago. We began in our living room with our roommates, Joshon and Taylor Miller. We didn't know what we were doing at all. We had all been discipled well and our affections had been won by Jesus. We knew he had transformed our thinking and our hearts. We knew we loved our city and we knew Jesus was the only hope for it.

In our initial whiteboard sessions, we discussed the commands of Jesus and what we wanted this community to be about: Jesus' love to us, in us, and through us. We desperately wanted show people God's love and proclaim the gospel with our words and actions. We wanted to be part of brining the kingdom of God to our part of the city.

Over the last several years, we've seen communities engage unengaged neighborhoods with the gospel through service, parties, foster care, friendship, and neighborly conversations. We've been able to send leaders to start communities that have gone on to do remarkable things. Through years of simply being present have fashion ed friendships that always dive into the spiritual. The stories are numerous of God's work through us, and we don't deserve it. However, what I'll cherish most is how we've experienced God's love.

What we weren't expecting, was to be transformed ourselves. With the streams of people coming and going, what has remained constant is God's gracious invitation to receive his love and direct our love to him.

This is my final challenge: engage the journey of discovering Jesus' sufficiency in mission and community. Grow to cherish his presence above communal accomplishments and missional engagement. That's when it really becomes fun.

APPENDIXES

Digital downloads of all appendixes and many other resources and tools available for free at: www.senttogether.org

APPENDIX I: MISSIONAL COMMUNITY LEADERS' ROLE DESCRIPTION

QUALIFICATIONS OF A LEADER

- Motivated by the gospel. It seems like a given, but many leaders can lead for other reasons.
- Have a desire to help others grow in faith and obedience by pointing them to Jesus.
- Committed to the long process of helping others grow in faith and obedience. It will take time and will not feel great or exciting most of the time.
- Prayerful and dependent on God. The Holy Spirit dwells within you. God is your helper that empowers you to love others. Leaders are those who pray and listen to the Spirit.
- Servants to Jesus as Lord. You are not building your resumé or gaining God's approval by leading a community. Instead, you are selflessly serving Jesus.
- Honest with their own mess as they repent and believe the gospel. Leaders who are honest and open about their struggles to believe the gospel.
- Understands they can't make people change. Leaders are faithful in sharing the gospel and trying new things, they are also quick to turn to God in prayer and learn from others.
- Submitted to elders of the church. This means they consider with great weight what elders have to say and do not view themselves as lone rangers.

PRACTICES OF A LEADER

As a leader, you will point people to the gospel in the Bible, speak the gospel in your own words, connect the gospel to people's stories, pray in light of the gospel, and call people to serve as demonstrations of the gospel. Leaders create an environment where community can happen.

- Pray for each individual in in your community.
- Process and think through the state of your community (this can happen in coaching, too).
    - Regularly ask how your people are doing as individuals and families? How are you all doing together?
    - Regularly pray and ask yourself what it looks like for your community to walk in repentance and faith? What does obedience look like for us? What is God calling us to?
- Share leadership. This means they trust others to lead in specific ways and makes times to get with the other leaders to process and plan.
- Regularly attends leadership huddles and retreats where they share in the learnings of other leaders.
- Connected to a coach who cares for them and helps them process all of the above.

TIME COMMITMENT OF A LEADER

Roughly 2 hours a week, outside your participation in the missional community you lead.

- 1 hour praying and processing. As you will likely see a lot of time is spent thinking about and praying for the people in your community. You are also asked to think about the current state of your community and where God is leading you forward.
- 1 hour preparing or planning. This might mean preparing for discussions, planning meetings, planning missional engagement, etc. This will also likely look like time with coaches and leadership meetings.

APPENDIX II: LEADERSHIP ASSESSMENT CHECKLIST

This assessment not an exam to pass, but a process to walk through for your own growth. You are seeking to understand how God has wired you *and* how you will need to be dependent on him and others as you lead. The person asking the questions should ask questions seeking stories: "how has this 'topic' worked itself out in your life recently?"

Furthermore, as you walk through this assessment, it will directly fit into your leadership development plan. First, fill this out on your own. Then have a close friend or spouse do it. Then, have an elder or leader in your church sit down with you as well.

VISION, HOPES, AND UNDERSTANDING OF HEALTH
[ ] Can you articulate what a healthy missional community looks like?
[ ] What would a missional community look like in your neighborhood? How would it be different from others?
[ ] What are the challenges facing a missional community for you?
[ ] What do you hope your missional community will look like?

YOUR LEADERSHIP AND AWARENESS
[ ] Do people follow you?
[ ] Do you have an understanding on what you're responsible for?
[ ] Do you understand your leadership style?
[ ] What makes you a good leader?
[ ] What makes you a bad leader?
[ ] What help do you know you will need as you lead?
[ ] How do you deal with conflict?
[ ] How do you attempt to cope with stress?

HEAD - KNOWLEDGE AND UNDERSTANDING

[ ] What is the gospel, in your own words?
[ ] What is the mission?
[ ] How does God save people?
[ ] How does the gospel transform us?
[ ] How does the gospel move us?
[ ] Can you offer a reason for the hope you have?
[ ] How do you doubt or wrestle with God?

HEART - CHARACTER AND SPIRITUAL LIFE

[ ] How do you make time to pray?
[ ] How do you sabbath (rest&delight in God's work)?
[ ] How do you become aware of the condition of your heart?
[ ] How has God broth you to repentance and faith?
[ ] What will be your biggest temptation as a leader?
[ ] What motivates you to start a community?
[ ] How do you depend on the Spirit instead of controlling with your own abilities?
[] Are you teachable, do you easily listen to others?
[] How do you ask for help? Is that hard?

HANDS - OBEDIENCE, SKILL, PRACTICE

[ ] How do you make disciples?
[ ] How do you teach others to seek God in prayer, study, worship?
[ ] How do you help others love others in words&deed?
[ ] How will you explain the gospel for others?
[ ] What 'responsibility' of leadership are you most confident in?
[ ] What 'responsibility' of leadership are you least confident in?

APPENDIX III: A LEADERSHIP DEVELOPMENT PLAN

PERSONAL HOPE&DREAM FOR MISSIONAL COMMUNITY

Get with your co-leaders and leaders in training to think through this first section together.

A Missional Community exists because of the gospel. We are growing up into a deeper understanding and application of the gospel. We are taking the gospel to the neighborhood, city, and world through intentional missional engagement.

1. What would your Missional Community look like if it was thriving?

2. What would your neighborhood look like if it knew Jesus? What If they saw the transformation Jesus brings to a community of people?

3. What would you like to see happen this year in your MC?

4. What are goals that would move your community to take a few steps forward toward your MC vision?

LEADING A MISSIONAL COMMUNITY

In light of those hopes, dreams, and goals, use this section to explore what your role is in leading this missional community. What is your role in leading your MC?

5. What areas do you feel like you need to grow in to lead your community?

PERSONAL DEVELOPMENT

Leaders are examples in communities of people who are walking in repentance and faith. They are growing in their knowledge of the gospel, belief in the gospel, and obedience to the gospel. One helpful way to think about this transformation is in terms of our head, heart, and hands being conformed to the image of Christ. As you work through this section, look for themes and connections across each area.

Head: Growing in Knowledge

"And do not be conformed to this world, but be transformed by the renewing of your mind, so that you may prove what the will of God is, that which is good and acceptable and perfect." — Romans 12:2

6. Where do you need to grow in knowledge? Are there things you need to know? Is there an issue you need to press into, an issue of Scripture to grow in deeper understanding of? Are there pieces of theology you need to learn? Are there aspects of gospel communities on mission that you still need to know?

7. How will you learn? (i.e. Is there a book or article to read, equipping session you need to attend, commentaries or studies to do, scripture to memorize, etc.?)

Heart: Growing in Belief

"I pray that the eyes of your heart may be enlightened, so that you will know what is the hope of His calling, what are the riches of the glory of His inheritance in the saints." — Ephesians 1:18

8. What areas of life do you need to grow in belief in the gospel? What areas do you need to see repentance in? What bondage are you volunteering for in your heart? What forgiveness needs to happen?

9. How will you grow in belief? (i.e. Shepherding conversations to have, questions and issues to bring up in discipleship and accountability groups, what material do you need to walk through, Redemption Immersion, prayer, fasting, retreats, etc.?)

Hands: Growing in Obedience, Skill, Practice.

"Teaching them to obey everything I have commanded." — Matthew 28:20
"Being no hearer who forgets but a doer who acts." — James 1:22-25
"Jesus glorified the Father by accomplishing the work he gave him to do." — John 17:4

10. What skills do you need practice in? Where are you excelling and need to keep growing at? Where are you failing to live what you believe? What skills do you need to develop? What things is God calling you to that you need to step into in obedience?

11. How will you grow in obedience, skill, and practice? (i.e. Are there trainings to attend, do you need to shadow someone, do you need to make a schedule, schedule some specific coaching to help you, are there opportunities for practice and feedback you need to pursue?)

APPENDIX IV: STARTING A MISSIONAL COMMUNITY CHECKLIST

BIG PICTURE AND LEADERSHIP
[ ] Vision, hopes, and dreams for this Missional Community
[ ] Missional Leader(s)
[ ] Shepherding Leader(s)
[ ] Common Mission
[ ] Plan for first baby step into common mission
[ ] Plan for first 8 to 10 weeks to lay gospel foundation
[ ] Coach or mentor to support and encourage
[ ] A "core" committed to the process

RESPONSIBILITIES
[ ] Host(s)
[ ] Meal Planner
[ ] Prayer Person

DETAILS/PLANNING
[ ] Date/Time to start and for regular meetings
[ ] Decide on food scheduling
[ ] Decide how you to communicate - text, Facebook, e-mail, etc.

EARLY DAYS AFTER LAUNCH
[ ] Name for your missional community
[ ] Grow in understanding of the mission
[ ] Share life stories
[ ] Discuss how you will include and care for children

APPENDIX V: A MONTH IN THE LIFE OF A MISSIONAL COMMUNITY

The best way to plan and lead your community is to think in months and *then* weeks. Planning week-to-week is too exhausting, especially for the busy leader. There is too much to think through and everything comes quickly in the normal rhythm of life. When leaders plan week-to-week their intentionality becomes nearly non-existent, and their organization tends to fall apart. The weeks become disconnected. The movement of the community *towards* something stalls.

It is better to do the bulk of the planning month-to-month. You can plan it all out with balance, then you can move forward preparing for each week. Planning monthly also gives the entire community a heads up, so they can plan their lives accordingly.

KNOW THE "SEASON" YOU'RE IN

The time of year, season of life, and all the factors affecting your city are affecting your community. Plan accordingly. For example, in the summer, everyone might be in and out while on vacation. However, during the summer there are greater opportunities to pursue relationships. Consider this in your planning. Or, are you approaching the holidays? How can your community grow in your love for one another through Thanksgiving and Christmas? How can you grow in loving God through Advent? How can you welcome others in and serve them during, what is for many, a difficult season.

In a similar way, consider the spiritual season your community is in. Are you deeply intrenched in caring for a burden of one of your members? Is there a growth towards prayer that is happening? How should your plan respond to that? Is there a resistance to repentance or dealing with sin? What is God calling your community to grow in?

126

LEAD IN BALANCE THE AIMS OF MISSIONAL COMMUNITY

Your community is seeking to grow in it's love for God (gospel enjoyment), love for one another (community), and love for city (mission). This ought to be expressed through your monthly calendar. The goal of planning monthly is to outline when and how will your community grow in each of these things. You simply can't do all these things every time your community gets together. They all bleed into each other, but your community will have to focus on one each time.

SHARE LEADERSHIP EASILY

Meet with your co-leaders towards the end of each month to pray for your community, debrief the past month, and plan the upcoming month. As you do this, assign who will be responsible for what based on their leadership roles. For example, the missional leader will lead the missional times, and the shepherding leader will lead the shepherding gatherings. These meetings will be truly life-giving.

SEEK INPUT FROM COACH

Ask your coach to help you plan each month in the beginning. As you get a feel for leadership, ask your coach to critique your plan. After you are confident, consider how you can help others begin and lead communities. This template can be a great format for coaching conversations.

EXAMPLE OF A MONTHLY PLAN

Prayer for the month: See our complete need for the gospel as we seek to help those overwhelmed by the needs of others.

Week 1: Focus: Gospel Enjoyment/Community.
Meal where focus is confession and repentance (Jared leads). Later in the week have a 'game-night' (hosted by the Wilsons).

Week 2: Focus: Mission.
Do a babysitting night for foster families in your neighborhood (Stacey organizes). Later in the week, encourage everyone to take a day of rest as individuals and families over the weekend. (John will share some sabbath resources via e-mail.)

Week 3: Focus: Gospel Enjoyment
Meal where focus is on studying scriptures (Jared Leads). Later in the week go to a happy hour in the neighborhood where you can invite friends and co-workers.

Week 4: Focus: Mission
Meet to put care packages together for case-workers and foster families and thank them for loving and caring for children (Caleb organizes). Later in the week, a few folks will deliver them.

TEMPLATE OF A MONTHLY PLAN

Prayer for Month: _____

Week 1: Focus _____
What? _____ Who Leads? _____
Later in the Week?

Week 2: Focus _____
What? _____ Who Leads? _____
Later in the Week?

Week 3: Focus _____
What? _____ Who Leads? _____
Later in the Week?

Week 4: Focus _____
What? _____ Who Leads? _____
Later in the Week?

APPENDIX VI: A "NORMAL" MISSIONAL COMMUNITY MEAL

How can this weekly meeting become more than just an agenda item on everyone's planner? How is it more than just a 'thing' you lead?

The weekly missional community meeting is the "garden plot" of missional leadership. A weak or disorganized weekly gathering produces similar results. An intense and over structured meeting can suck the life out of what should be a relational time of saints and skeptics with God at the center. This meeting is the foundational building block of community. All the hopes and aspirations for life outside that time will flow from this structured time. The liturgy of your community is not logistics but worship planning.

What do you include? How much is too much? This is a simple guide to what a typical community gathering looks like. Within each element you will find ample room for creativity and intentionality. My prayer is that the Holy Spirit animates each moment and the gospel is made clear through each activity.

BEFORE THE NIGHT

Believe it or not, there is work to be done before everyone arrives at the host home or gathering spot. Here are three crucial steps to be done each week.

Planning

As the leaders you have to plan out the purpose of that week's meeting. What will be the 1 big goal you have for that time? What will be necessary? How will you pursue that goal in the limited time your community has together? How can everyone prepare?

This weekly purpose is most easily done by thinking about the entire month. Toward the end of the month, plan out the next week-by-week and how each week fits with the other, who will lead each week, etc. This really alleviates leadership stress!

Communication

Tell everyone in the group what the plan is for the evening. What the focus will be, what you will be doing, and what to bring for food. Try to communicate early in the week so no one has to run to the store at the last minute to bring a dish. This is where a good communications person who thinks ahead is really helpful.

Preparation

The person leading the intentional time will need to prepare to lead. The host needs to prepare the home. Each participate needs to prepare their hearts and food to share. The leaders pray. A community has to prepare itself to experience community.

GATHERING&EATING – 1 HOUR

The weekly meeting begins through arrival or gathering. This is the moment when everyone's individual responsibilities, schedules, and to-do lists collide into an expression of community. The worries, struggles, fears, and happy news of each member comes rushing through the door. Your lives are hurried until this point. Your lives are physically separate until this moment. A weekly meal is more than a logistic to work out but a spiritual discipline of being united. You are physically united by the table you gather around, the complete meal everyone shares in, and under the prayer recognizing God's grace as you eat.

Furthermore, this is more than a Christian dinner party. It is a gathering of those lunging toward belief in Christ. Through the meal we engage one another as family in Christ and we engage Christ. This is a fantastic space to grow in your love for one another. Let the conversations around the dinner table be focused and important. Embrace this moment with honesty. As a leader, spark the conversation to be about more than the movies people watch and the latest sports scores.

Tips for Making This Time Meaningful:

- Ask each other how the week is going and expect long honest answers.
- Ask everyone a common question that will lead to deeper understanding of each other: What is your favorite summer memory from childhood? Or how do you prepare for the Christmas holidays.
- Ask about how each person is processing the sermon from Sunday, or about the service that was done as a group the week before, circle back to past hardships people have shared.
- Simple things to like what are you thankful for today. What was the hardest part of your day today?
- You could also have a person or couple in the "spotlight" where they are able to share in more depth their story, current spot in life, and what they are going through with the community having the chance to pray for them.

TRANSITION&ANNOUNCEMENTS – 10 MINUTES

After the meal, you will transition to a more focused time that isn't interrupted by the eating and excitement of getting together. Believe it or not, transitioning from the lively and sporadic conversation of the table to the pointed purpose of the gathering is the most difficult part of leading a community. This is when you're anxiety of pleasing people will come through. This is when control takes over. This is when leaders often lose track of time. This has always been my biggest struggle.

One of the best ways to signal a shift in gathering is with announcements, which have to be shared anyway. You want to have a time when the community can communicate about the life happening outside. This is the time to share about upcoming opportunities to serve others, parties where to invite neighbors, what's happening in the church as a whole, and even the upcoming meal plans. This is also the chance to ask everyone: "What's coming up with you in the next couple weeks?"

Tips for Transitions:

These things help create a clear marker and shift in the evening.
- Dismiss the children to their activities and time (if this is something your community has decided to do).
- Clean up from dinner
- Actually move from sitting at the table to sitting in the living room.

INTENTIONAL&FOCUSED TIME – 45 MINUTES

You have gathered from separate lives and brought your lives into unity over a meal. You have discussed how your life together will spill out into other arenas through announcements. Now it is time to do something together. For a precious 40 minutes your community will share the spiritual practices of learning to following Jesus. You will do this together. This is special.

Will this be an evening when your community will do something to grow in it's love for Christ together? In it's love for neighbor?   Here are just a few ideas of things you could do. However, this is a space to be creative and your ideas will be better for you than mine because they will be yours.

Growing in Our Love for Christ Together:

- A time of communal prayer, weekly Examen or Lectio Divina.
- A time of reading and studying the Scriptures together.
- A time of confession on where we are with struggles, belief/doubt, mission, relationships, or simply following Jesus. This would be followed by a time of confessing God's faithfulness.
- A time of repentance and faith through singing, artwork, discussion, or some other creative way to worship God together.

Growing in Our Love for the City Together:

- A time of prayer for those in your common mission.
- A planning meeting where your community plans how it will engage the poor and vulnerable in a concerted way. Not theoretical but tangible: who is going to bring what, who will be there, how can those who aren't there support the others.
- Discussion on what gifts, skills, or resources your community has to offer.
- Plan a party or event you can invite friends, family, and co-workers to join in.
- Have a conversation about what your community is learning about itself while on mission and about people. What has been challenging.

SCATTERING&SENDING – 2 MINUTES

Then comes the moment when the evening is done and it is time to leave and re-scatter. Close your time together by praying for the lives you will now live physically separated but spiritually unified. Pray a commissioning prayer as your community leaves and goes their separate ways. Pray for the children, the parents, the students, the teachers, the entrepreneurs, the artists, etc, that they will be reconciled to Christ and that they will be an image of God and his grace. I have far too often missed this opportunity. I am also terrible and bringing meetings to a clear conclusion. Here is a good example of this sort of communal benediction I found in the Celtic Daily Prayer Book:

"May the peace of Christ go with us, where ever he may send us,

May he guide us through the wilderness, protect us through the storms.

May he bring us together rejoicing at the wonders he has shown us.

May he bring us home rejoicing once again through these doors."

AFTER THE NIGHT

Following the time together it is typically a good idea to have the "communication" person send out a quick message on what was discussed and planned so people can remember and for those that missed the time. This is a thoughtful way to include those who are unable to come.

TEMPLATE OF A WEEKLY MEETING

GATHERING&EATING – 1 HOUR
Food Plan:

TRANSITION&ANNOUNCEMENTS – 10 MIN.
Announcements:

INTENTIONAL&FOCUSED TIME – 45 MINUTES
What will be the focus: Inward or Outward?

What will we do?

Who will lead?

What needs to be prepared?

SCATTERING&SENDING – 2 MINUTES
Who will pray for us as we scatter?

APPENDIX VII: EXAMPLE OF A MISSIONAL COMMITMENT

ALLANDALE/CRESTVIEW MISSIONAL COMMUNITY

By Gods grace we are a missional community in the Allandale/Crestview neighborhood. Because of the gospel of Jesus we want to grow in our devotion to him, to one another, and to our neighbors and city.

Devotion to Jesus

By Gods grace we commit to growing in our devotion to Jesus by:

- Gathering with the other MCs on Sundays for worship and gospel teaching.
- Gathering on Tuesday evenings for dinner, discussion, and prayer focused on the gospel. (X will organize meal/childcare schedule, X will lead discussion, X will write down and send out prayer requests).
- Read Paul E. Miller's *The Praying Life* together and discuss.
- Attending a Parenting Seminar together.

Devotion to One Another

By Gods grace we commit to growing in our devotion to one another by:

- Committing to regularly pray for, encourage, and forgive one another.
- Establishing an "emergency fund" (overseen by two capable leaders) so that we can help any of us who is unexpectedly in a financial crisis.
- Having a monthly "Sunday Night Family Dinner" together. Also, open to friends and neighbors. (Organized by X).

- The men in our group will regularly check on single mom to see how we can help her as a single mother.(i.e. yard work, heavy lifting, etc).
- Faithfully encourage X through his battle with cancer through prayer, regular visits, and providing meals via a care calendar.

Devotion to Our Neighbor and City

By Gods grace we commit to growing in our devotion to our neighbors and city by:

- We feel we have been sent to the Allandale/Crestview neighborhoods, in particular, the people we regularly interact with in our neighborhoods, Gullet Elementary, and Lamar Middle School.
- We plan to regularly be present and to serve at the local schools: specifically painting the parent resource room at Lamar Middle School, volunteering at the LamarFest, sponsoring the end of year sports banquet, and pursuing other opportunities to serve the community. X will organize the serve opportunities with the schools since they have kids attending.
- We will regularly pray as a group for our neighbors and friends who do not know and believe the good news of Jesus.
- We will host bi-monthly parties that we intentionally invite our neighbors to.
- We will serve regularly with X as a way of serving the working poor and single parent families in Wooten Park, and inviting our neighbors to serve with us so they can see the gospel expressed in love for the poor.

Digital downloads of all appendixes and many other resources and tools available for free at: www.senttogether.com

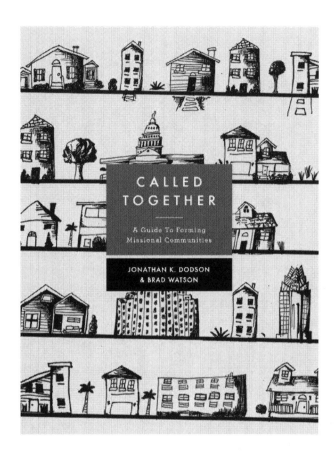

This eight week guide helps communities discover their calling to be and make disciples together. The eight weeks covers important discussions on the gospel, community, and mission while also giving communities next steps to practice what they've talked about. Available at www.gcdiscipleship.com and amazon.com.

FURTHER READING

THE GOSPEL
Gospel-Centered Discipleship by Jonathan Dodson
The King Jesus Gospel by Scott McKnight
Prodigal God by Timothy Keller
Simply Jesus by N.T. Wright
You Can Change by Tim Chester

COMMUNITY
Everyday Church by Steve Timmis and Tim Chester
Life Together by Dietrich Bonhoeffer
When the Church Was A Family by Joseph Hellerman

MISSION
The Mission of God by Christopher Wright
A Meal With Jesus by Tim Chester
Saturate by Jeff Vanderstelt

LEADERSHIP
In the Name of Jesus by Henri Nouwen
Under the Unpredictable Plant by Eugene Peterson
Leaders Eat Last by Simon Sinek

ABOUT THE AUTHOR

Brad Watson (M.A. in Theology) serves as a pastor at Bread&Wine Communities in Portland, OR. As a member of the planting team, Brad has helped coach, train, and start missional communities throughout the city. One of his greatest passions is helping leaders realize the dreams and calling God has given them for community and mission.

Brad is a regular contributor at WeAreSoma.com, TheVergeNetwork.com, and GospelCenteredDiscipleship.com. He is also co-author of *Raised? Finding Jesus by Doubting the Resurrection* (Zondervan 2014) and *Called Together: A Guide to Forming Missional Communities* (GCD Books 2014).

Brad lives in inner southeast Portland with his wife, Mirela, and their two daughters.

You can read more of his work at bradawatson.com and download free resources for missional communities leaders,and coaching at senttogether.org.

OTHER GCD RESOURCES

Visit GCDiscipleship.com

THE STORIES WE LIVE

*Discovering the True and Better
Way of Jesus.*

SEAN POST
Foreword by *RICK MCKINLEY*

"The Bible as a whole is a story, a grand narrative, that grips our hearts, our minds, our imaginations. We join with Jesus and His community on a quest which demands our best effort in the team's mission. The end is glorious indeed. *The Stories We Live* is a great introduction to that grand narrative and also some of the broken stories which distract many. Read, be gripped by the story, and join the quest!"

Gerry Breshears, Professor of Theology,
Western Seminary, Portland, OR

Make, Mature, Multiply aims to help you become a disciple who truly understands the full joy of following Jesus. With a wide range of chapters from some of today's most battle-tested disciple-makers, this book is designed for any Christian seeking to know more about being a fully-formed disciple of Jesus who makes, matures, and multiplies fully-formed disciples of Jesus.

everPresent

HOW THE GOSPEL RELOCATES US IN THE PRESENT

By Jeremy Writebol

Foreword by Jonathan Dodson

"*everPresent* does something that most books don't achieve. Most focus either on who God is or what we should do. Jeremy starts with who God is to walk the reader down the path of what God has done, who we are because of God, then points us to understand what we do because of this. I highly recommend picking up *everPresent* to better understand the why and how of the life of those that follow Jesus."

Seth McBee, Executive Team Member, GCM Collective

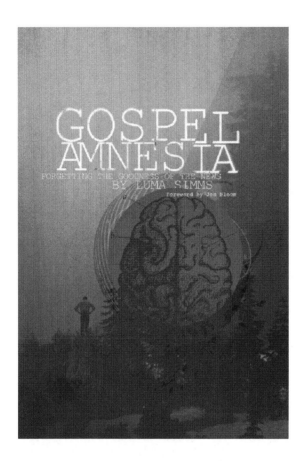

"Luma Simms remembers vividly what it was like to be simply going through the motions of a spiritual life. She writes like someone who has just been awakened from a nightmare and can still describe it in detail. Luma's voice communicates the pain of forgetting what matters most, and may be just the voice to reach the half-awake."

Fred Sanders, Associate Professor of Theology, Torrey Honors Institute, Biola University and author of Jesus in Trinitarian Perspective and Wesley on the Christian Life

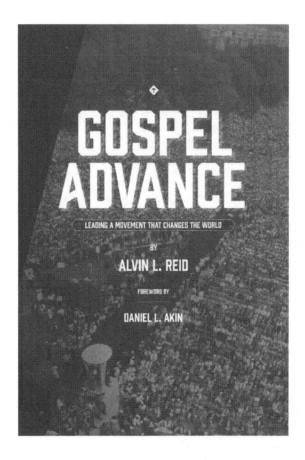

"*Gospel Advance* is Alvin Reid's challenge to the Church to recover our mission focus and advance a movement of God through the gospel. Reading this book is like sitting down across from this passionate evangelism professor and hearing from his heart. May the Lord use this work to ignite your heart for the nations!"

Trevin Wax, Managing Editor of *The Gospel Project*

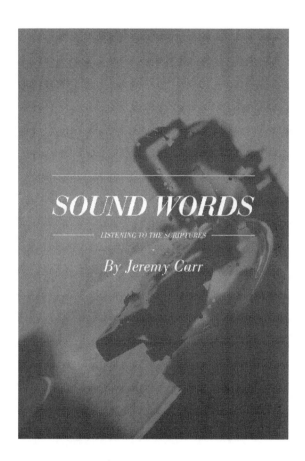

SOUND WORDS

LISTENING TO THE SCRIPTURES

By Jeremy Carr

"The church continues to need an understanding of discipleship that draws people to love and know God. This book delivers. It is an accessible and practical theology of scripture for discipleship. Jeremy is not exhorting you to love the Bible more, but declaring that God's love for you causes you to know and love him and his Word more."

Justin S. Holcomb, Adjunct Professor of Theology and *Philosophy, Reformed Theological Seminary and co-author of God Mae All of Me: A Book to Help Children Protect Their Bodies*

Made in the USA
San Bernardino, CA
07 March 2016